Hol

We acknowledge The Estate of P.K. Page for permission to quote from the writings of P.K. Page and to reproduce images of her visual art.

Caitlin Press Inc.
3375 Ponderosa Way
Qualicum Beach, BC V9K 2J8
www.caitlinpress.com

Text and cover design by Vici Johnstone
Edited by Yvonne Blomer and DC Reid
Artwork by P.K. Irwin

Printed in Canada

Caitlin Press Inc. acknowledges financial support from the Government of Canada and the Canada Council for the Arts, and the Province of British Columbia through the British Columbia Arts Council and the Book Publisher's Tax Credit. Library and Archives Canada Cataloguing in Publication

Canada Council   Conseil des Arts   BRITISH COLUMBIA   Funded by the   Canada
for the Arts   du Canada   ARTS COUNCIL   Government
                                                          of Canada

Title: Hologram : homage to P.K. Page / edited by Yvonne Blomer & DC Reid.
Other titles: Hologram (2023)
Names: Blomer, Yvonne, editor. | Reid, D. C. (Dennis C.), 1952- editor.
Description: Poems.
Identifiers: Canadiana 20230477100 | ISBN 9781773861135 (softcover)
Subjects: LCSH: Canadian poetry—20th century. | CSH: Canadian Poetry (English)—20th century. |
  LCGFT: Poetry.
Classification: LCC PS8293.1 .H65 2023 | DDC C811/.608—dc23

Hologram

Homage to P.K. Page
edited by Yvonne Blomer & DC Reid

Caitlin Press 2023

Though sickness and death take their terrible toll
and they did and they do—one's astonishing heart
almost sings through its grief like a bird—water bird—
in the wind and waves of some vast salty sea.
Explain it? I can't. But it's true I'm in love
with some point beyond sight, with some singular star
for which words won't suffice, which reduce it, in fact.

P.K. Page, *Hand Luggage*

Our feet barely touched the earth, and memory
erased at birth, but gradually reassembling
coalesced and formed a whole, as single birds
gathering for migration form a flock.

P.K. Page, "Presences"

Contents

DC Reid on P.K. Page

P.K. Page Trust Fund for Mentoring

At the time of P.K. Page's passing early in 2010, in a room filled with family and friends, along with fifty poets, many also friends, it crossed my mind that it would be good to have something tangible to remember her by. Closely thereafter, I asked Marilyn Bowering, who was a closer friend than I, whether a mentoring program in her name would be a good focus for a fundraising purpose to both remember her and to benefit Canadian poets.

Marilyn responded, saying: "Although P.K. is not known to have used the word 'mentorship' when describing her relationship to other poets, it is what she stood for. She supported, advocated for, arranged meetings between, fostered community among and wrote letters for poets she believed in. Often these were younger poets, but not always. She had an eye out for the talented and overlooked and quietly, in the background, offered literary, social and sometimes financial support."

I had just allowed myself to be talked into being president at the League of Canadian Poets, mostly, on my part, so I could create some financial benefits for poets. I decided that the League would be a good place to mount a mentorship program to benefit those starting out and those with many books already published. This conviction started what turned out to be a decade's long journey of raising enough money, and donating just as much, to get the fund to almost $50,000 in 2020.

TD bank's minimum was a $10,000 investment. In 2011, several of us donated to start the fund. P.K.'s son Neal Irwin and brother Michael Page donated $1,000 each, while I and Roger Nash donated $2,000 each. And before the end of the year, I put together a P.K. Page Trust Fund reading in Victoria, as well as published a book of the poems read, and raised an additional $2,300. Along with this, 8–12 readings were allocated to members who donated their fees, and that pushed us over the bar. Other League members have held readings to raise funds, for example, John Barton and Jay Ruzesky, both in this book.

For *Hologram: Homage to P.K. Page* we asked poets to write poems related to P.K., whether inspired by a quote, poems, glosas, and versions of glosas, as well we asked for stories of how they may have been mentored/influenced by P.K. (all poets know her as P.K., rather than Patricia Kathleen) over the years. There are revealing and touching stories throughout this book. And an ekphrastic poem or two. The chosen poets received a copy of this book, and my own book of "amended" glosas, *The Spirit of the Thing and the Thing Itself.*

To complement the written part of the book, Zailig Pollock, P.K.'s literary executor, graciously allowed us to use almost twenty of P.K. Irwin's paintings (her name as a visual artist was her husband's last name: Irwin) and we have tried to place them with poems that have some resemblance to the often-luminous pieces.

~

Now, I want to tell you more about P.K. and how mentorship influenced her art, both poetry and visual, and how she influenced me and others. The words mentor and mentee were not related with poetry until the 1990s but digging into her story makes it clear P.K. was both a mentor and mentee since the late 1930s. And her raw talent at painting is almost stunning when you look at her *Birthday Card for Daddie*, painted when she was four years old, as in preternaturally talented.

I discussed her story and art with Zailig Pollock, Sandra Djwa, author of the Governor General's award-winning P.K. biography, *Journey with No Maps: A Life of P.K. Page*, and Michèle Rackham Hall, author of *The Art of P.K. Irwin: observer, other, Gemini.* I also reread their books and highly recommend them. Each was good enough to write pieces on their areas of special interest, and you will find them within this editorial section. Michèle, along with Zailig wrote captions for each image. Through these three, what emerged was Page's life and association with many mentors over the many decades.

Now, P.K.'s story: while she was every bit as creative as the rest in her Montreal poetry group, *Preview,* in the 1930s and 1940s, and accepted as an equal, she was in the company of men as much as sixteen years older than her, and the natural structure for passing on things learned with a longer poetry background—as in mentors. This is the era when F.R. Scott was the lead and he became both a poetry influencer as well as a long-term, deep romance.

Soon after this period, P.K.'s poetry books were being devoured by a generation of new, women, writers. For example, in *Journey With no Maps,* Sandra Djwa quotes Alice Munro, who was working at Munro's Book Store, the iconic place to pick up a book in Victoria, when P.K. walked in, and, in conversation, mentioned she was a writer and added her name. Alice went pale and then blushed deeply because P.K. was an icon to her. She thought she might faint.

Other writers were also influenced by P.K.'s guiding hand. Margaret Atwood was also a great admirer: "P.K.'s importance as poet, cultural figure, and inspiration to many younger poets cannot be overestimated," from *Journey with No Maps*.

Margaret had spent the late 1950s at the University of Toronto reading Page in her scruffy rooms. She found some of her images "blew the top of my head off." This was the late fifties, in an era where women were not so easily inserted into the writing world.

For a time, many of the two poets' poems bore resemblance to one another. In one of them, P.K.'s poem "Element," her influence is easily seen. The woman protagonist is portrayed as injured, and compared with a fish, on a hook who is "silently hurt—it's mouth alive with metal." In Atwood's writing, this was revealed in the wildly painful, well-known image from *Power Politics*:

you fit into me
like a hook into an eye

a fish hook
an empty eye.

The mentorship influence of P.K. extended to a new generation, including Marilyn Bowering, Patricia Young, Michael Ondaatje, and, later, influenced me to write a book of glosas from her lead in *Hologram*. "Her incredibly high standards, [were] coupled with great kindness to younger writers," said Sandra Djwa in a *Malahat Review* interview.

P.K. soon discovered, through Ivan Serpa's teaching, etching, oil paint and egg tempera. And at Serpa's suggestion, she embraced her artistic life, rather than written. The tools of the trade, such as papers, paints and implements, she learned from Frank Shaeffer. But she broke with the latter because he had to her mind a too rational, rules-following method, where her mind wanted to charge everywhere and reach the sky.

Arthur was posted to New York in 1959, a year when the old world was relinquishing its hold on the art centre of the world, Paris; and artists were fleeing the broken continent, flooding New York, the new world centre of art. The Solomon R. Guggenheim Museum opened that year and solidified New York's reputation. And it was her great fortune to be there and meet some of her important art mentors.

Also, years later in *Hand Luggage*, P.K. was to say of Seliger that he "offered this pupil a pearl of great price / when he emphasized, water and oil never mix." She had finally found a teacher of authentic worth to her. Irwin began painting in oil gouache, then letting it dry. Then she applied the oil glaze that she brushed over with a wet brush before it dried, showing the layers below. It gave her art a luminosity she had sought. And felt that the two "saw with one eye," *Hand Luggage*.

Leonora Carrington became a close friend. Their shared gender and age allowed them to talk effectively. And Carrington never acted as critic, a male tendency. P.K. was to say: "she opened doors / and I walked through," *Journey with No Maps*. And also passed on a long list of artistic techniques and glazes. Carrington's method of tempera and how to use it led to a breakthrough for P.K., "it is like working hand in hand with the Holy Ghost."

In this *Hologram: Homage to P.K. Page*, you will find numerous examples of amended glosa forms, by many poets, myself included. This was a whole new world from the diplomatic circuit, to live in Victoria, a much smaller 'metropolitan' world than she had lived, and she was depressed in the early years here.

It was in this era, that P.K. Page became a mentor for generations of Canadian women writers, and which was followed by a wide range of examples, as this anthology clearly demonstrates. Canadian poets picked up from the bright examples of her sharp, silver images. And their stories of her influence are wide and varied. Read this book.

Years ago, I had P.K. read at Glenlyon Norfolk School. In introducing P.K., and her bright, patrician bearing, I made the comparison of her with the movie star I thought she most resembled, Audrey Hepburn. With her hands pointing down on either side of her hips, a commanding pose we all had come to know, she lifted her hands to either side of my face and gave me a big kiss on my lips. I was so surprised I fell off the stage. Well, I mentally fell off and climbed back to hand her the mic and stagger off stage.

There is another thing about what she taught, without ever saying it: poems that start from work that the poet likes most, makes the poet rise up and write to that quality. That is mentorship, too. I changed from my style of being associative and elusive to strict formalism, meaning that P.K. enlarged my oeuvre, a great gift.

One poem is about a cougar. He had ripped saplings in a row down a wild road, beaten them to sticks, then covered them with blood red scent. I passed twenty-five blood red wet poles, ripped from the ground—such strength—before going down into a dry wash on my way to the Eve River. When I lifted my eyes, there was the male cougar at the far end of the gravel. I cleared my throat, and he began running directly for me. I didn't give it a second's thought and began running directly toward him. As we came together, eyes locked on one another, the cougar slid into the forest and was gone. A magical, dangerous moment for me, and because I think of felines as sexual in movement, the final line that came out of the blue was: "touch me I'm so beautiful," a perfect, gorgeous line, that I have P.K. to thank for and then an entire formalist book.

Jacaranda Doors

1958, PRIVATE COLLECTION, VICTORIA, BC. FELT PEN AND GOUACHE.

Jacaranda Doors is one of a number of paintings in felt pen and gouache that P.K. painted of her palacette in Brazil. The domestic pieces are predominantly realistic renderings of the house's architectural features, and the gouache helped P.K. capture the bright, exotic colours of the interior space she was mostly confined to as the wife of the Canadian Ambassador in the 1950s.

Michèle Rackham Hall and Zailig Pollock

Portrait of the Poet as Artist: P.K. Irwin

P.K. Page is known as one of Canada's finest poets, but under her married name P.K. Irwin, she was also a gifted painter. Her paintings and drawings belong to collections of some of Canada's most prestigious art galleries, including the Art Gallery of Ontario and the National Gallery of Canada, and have featured in numerous international exhibitions. Moreover, she studied and exhibited with high profile modernist artists both in Canada and abroad. Although she mostly kept her writing and artist identities separate in name, she used "the same pen" for poetry and painting, as she herself put it.

P.K. always had a keen interest in the visual arts, and throughout her life she counted a number of artists among her closest friends, such as Maxwell Bates, Jori Smith, Leonora Carrington and Pat Martin Bates. Even from a very early age she showed great artistic promise, as in a set of crayon drawings she did at the age of four: *Birthday Card for Daddie* (1920, see page 51), which appears on the cover of *Metamorphosis*, the recent edition of her writings for children. Sandra Djwa notes in *Journey with No Maps: A Life of P.K. Page* (2012) that P.K. spent countless hours at the library as a young girl discovering "the strange world of Cubist painting, pointillism…" and modern sculpture. In her early twenties, she befriended a group of painters in New Brunswick, which included now prominent Canadian artists Jack Humphrey, Miller Brittain, and Ted Campbell, and in her thirties, her creative circle in Montreal included the painters Philip Surrey, Goodridge Roberts, Peggy Anderson, and Jori Smith (the latter two for whom P.K. occasionally served as model). She clearly had ample exposure to the visual arts throughout her young adult life, so the fact that P.K. did not seriously take up painting until she was almost in her forties is indeed a mystery.

However, visual art always played a prominent role in P.K.'s poetics. She frequently describes works of art in her poetry, as in "Ecce Homo," but other examples include an imaginary tapestry in "Arras," and a series of her own *Yellow People* paintings (1958, see page 24) in "The Yellow People in Metamorphosis." At the same time, P.K. illustrated at least one poem, "Images of Angels" in her painting "Angels" (1957), and in a couple cases paintings and poems share the same or similar titles—the painting (1964, see page 79) and the poem "Planet Earth," and the painting *Evening Dance* (see page 144) and the poem "Evening Dance of the Grey Flies." Moreover, her poems were always intensely visual. She is the most painterly of poets. For example, in "After Rain" she describes a rain-soaked clothesline:

> hung from one thin rib
> a silver web—
> its infant, skeletal, diminutive,
> now sagged with sequins, pulled ellipsoid,
> glistening

Interestingly, "After Rain" ends with P.K. expressing her dissatisfaction with her role as a poet: and not long afterwards, in Brazil, she abandoned poetry altogether for painting.

Although her pen ceased to write poetry in Brazil, P.K.'s time there was her most prolific as an artist—about a quarter of her paintings date from a period of about two years in Brazil. As her diaries show, P.K. was obsessed with drawing and painting during this time. At first she was entirely self-taught, using whatever materials came to hand—felt pens, as in *Fowl Yard* (1959, see page 97) and packing paper—but she soon began to seek out instruction and to explore different media (gouache in particular) and aesthetics.

P.K. started out primarily as a figurative artist in Brazil—painting the domestic space of the *palacete* where she resided, such as *Jacaranda Doors* (c. 1958, see page 19), still lifes, such as *Flowers and Phone* (c. 1958, see page 91), which appears on the cover of the recent edition of *Brazilian Journal*, and the exotic geography and architecture of her new surroundings. It was not long, however, before she began to find her way to abstraction, and the modernism so prominent in her poetry. First, she tried her hand at figurative abstraction, as in her *Yellow People* series. In one painting from this series, yellow faceless figures congregate around two separate cages containing a red bird and a blue bird, considerably more defined in their features than their human observers. The setting and context of the scene are obscure, but the figures' relative abstraction (when compared with the birds) and similar colouration to the cages suggest an ironic play on the issue of captivity depicted in the piece. Eventually, P.K. began to experiment with non-iconic abstraction, though mostly through sketches rather than fully worked up compositions. The mood of P.K.'s work in Brazil is predominantly celebratory. P.K. herself drew comparisons with Matisse and, especially, Dufy; the overall impression is of joyous spontaneity.

Given P.K.'s new-found artistic talent and interest in abstraction, the timing of her and Arthur's brief move in 1959 to New York City, where Arthur represented Canada at the United Nations, was nothing short of auspicious. The city had recently taken over from Paris as an art mecca, with artists such as Jackson Pollock, Willem de Kooning, Robert Motherwell, and Charles Seliger of the "New York School," as well as Mark Tobey and Morris Graves, leading the abstract expressionist movement there. P.K. not only admired their works on display at the city's various galleries—the Museum of Modern Art and the recently opened Guggenheim, for example—but also met Tobey, whose work impressed her greatly, and Charles Seliger at gallery parties that she attended. Eventually, Seliger became her teacher, and his impact on her art is evident in the intricate, biomorphic details layered into her works of this period and beyond. For example, her *Bright Fish* (1960, see page 134) etching (a medium she learned from Harry Sternberg at the Arts Student League that fall) exhibits the gestural and calligraphic lines of automatism, and a focus on the detailed complexity of the internal being, qualities characteristic of Seliger's own work. Although P.K. abandoned etching, preferring the spontaneity of drawing and painting instead, this expressive and detailed lineation persisted in her paintings and drawings for many years. The whimsy and experimentation so prominent in her work from Brazil and New York, however, all but faded from focus once P.K. moved to Mexico in 1960.

Although P.K. produced considerably fewer works in Mexico, they tended to be on a larger scale, technically more ambitious and often, though not always, quite dark, even frightening, such as *By the Wave Rising, by the Wave Breaking* (1961, see page 43). Under the influence and mentorship of Leonora Carrington, who was one of P.K.'s closest friends in Mexico, she experimented with media such as egg tempera, gesso, and gold leaf; and Carrington, a leading surrealist, encouraged P.K. in her own surrealistic tendencies, which had often been evident in her poetry but were almost entirely absent from her predominantly representative work in Brazil. One of the most impressive examples is the exuberant *The Dance* (1963, see page 164), inspired by a performance of Chinese opera. This painting in egg tempera was P.K.'s favourite, and until her death it hung over the fireplace in her home in Victoria. It now hangs over the fireplace in the Page-Irwin Colloquium room at Trent University. The emotional, as well as technical range of P.K.'s painting in the Mexico years went far beyond anything she had attempted before or would ever attempt again.

Mexico was a period of spiritual turmoil for P.K., eventually leading to her discovery of Sufism, which was to become the center of her spiritual and artistic life in the years to come.

Not long after returning to Canada, P.K. returned to poetry as well, a new kind of poetry influenced by Sufi masters, such as Rumi; and she turned to a new kind of painting, influenced by the abstract, geometric patterning characteristic of Islamic art. In stark contrast to the dynamism of her surrealistic work in Mexico, these essentially static works seem to be intended as objects of contemplation, as aids to spiritual exploration rather than as a form of personal expression. Examples are *Votive Tablet* (1972, see page 56) in the medium of egg tempera and gold leaf, which P.K. had learned from Leonora Carrington, and *Excalibur's Handle* (c. 1973, see page 156), which consists of a hole-punched gouache, a medium with which she experimented at the time.

Until the end of her life, P.K. continued with non-iconic abstraction, creating serene, mandala-like works of great beauty and serenity, such as an untitled pen and ink drawing from 2005. Once she returned to poetry, however, her visual art no longer played the same central role in her career as it had in Brazil and Mexico. Instead, art became complementary to her poetics, serving to illustrate and illuminate her verse in publications, such as *Cry Ararat!* (1967), and *The Glass Air* (1985), as P.K.'s two identities merged into her creative practice as poet-artist.

The Yellow People

1958, PRIVATE COLLECTION, TORONTO, ON. OIL ON BOARD.

The Yellow People is one of a series of at least four paintings, of varying media, featuring the yellow faceless figures. It follows her earlier painting *Angels* (1957), also including faceless figures, and the title suggests a connection to otherworldly subjects of her poem "The Yellow People in Metamorphosis." Written many years later (1972), the poem revisits these painterly figures with "chromosomes / and yellow genes / squeezed from a tube of cadmium" (*Kaleidoscope*, 125).

Sandra Djwa

P.K. Page and Journey with No Maps

I first met P.K. Page's poetry in 1963 through selections reprinted in the Klinck and Watters' *Canadian Anthology*. In April 1970, I met her in person at Simon Fraser University when she came to speak to my Canadian poetry class. At first glance we did a double take because we both wore shades of purple, "blending in," as she put it, with SFU concrete panels of the same hue and consequently, in her view, "disappearing."

She was a vibrant presence, read beautifully, and my students were intrigued by the metaphysics of her poems. They had many questions, especially about her poem "Another Space." One of the students, Michele Preston, promptly wrote an honours essay on her poems and later prepared the first "Checklist" to Page's poetry. After her poetry reading, P.K. suggested that when I was next in Victoria, I should come to visit her and her husband, Arthur Irwin. Subsequently, when P.K. came to Vancouver to speak at various functions, she would sometimes phone and ask me to drive her around. On one of these occasions, circa 1986, she recalled a dream about her father, an imposing figure on a high horse. We talked about the dream and its meaning to her: clearly, she was beginning to think biographically. For over two decades, we were in regular contact, especially before and after the publication of my biography of F.R. Scott, *The Politics of the Imagination* (1987). Both Arthur and P.K. were very helpful regarding Ottawa life and the social circles in which they and the Scotts travelled.

I had encouraged P.K. to consider a biography. During one of my visits to Victoria in late 1995, she told me that *The Malahat Review* was planning a special edition for her eightieth birthday. In early January, 1996, she wrote: "You might like to do something for it and it might get us both used to the idea of further work." As she had said earlier in the same letter, a biography would be "better now [rather] than after I've lost my marbles or am dead. Also, now there are people alive who knew me when I was young." But she emphasized, "this is in no way a commitment." I couldn't write a full-fledged article as I was completing *Professing English*, a biography of the poet and academic Roy Daniells, but I did agree to do an interview. It turned out to be biographical in nature and P.K. and I sent letters back and forth, correcting where necessary, moving materials around. We were both pleased at the end of the collaboration. We had discovered we could talk and work together comfortably—the first essential for any biography.

P.K. had now come to the recognition that she was reaching the end of her creative life and she wanted help to record her achievements. Specifically, she wanted her biography written (although she liked to maintain that she did not) and her poems and short fiction collected. I suggested Zailig Pollock as editor of the poems and fiction on the basis of his splendid edition of A.M. Klein's poems, and P.K. happily agreed. But a biography raised large emotional issues. Aside from the question of what she wanted to disclose, there were at least three biographers available to write her life. Yet in our small Canadian literary world any choice might wound existing good feelings and friendships, so she occasionally fudged her decision. And she was very nervy about the biographical process itself. To some degree she felt it unseemly to want to have a biography. But like many biographical subjects, if a biography was going to be written, she wanted to tell her version of her story (which, of course, a biographer shouldn't do), and indeed she did tell it her way in several subsequent publications.

She telephoned to formally ask me to write her biography on December 21, 1996, drafted a summary contract on February 27, 1997, and followed this up with a letter of permission on October 14, 1997 saying that her biography would be "one in which you would be free to interpret as you see fit …You also know a great deal about the age in which I have lived …. I have total confidence in your painstaking research and ability to get on top of a body of material."

In retrospect, I think P.K. was a maverick in the original meaning of the term: sensitive, high-strung, often unwilling to run with the rest of the herd. Working with her was most often a pleasure. I think it would be truthful to say that we both enjoyed the process, some of her interview tapes are punctuated by laughter and the songs and sayings that we both remembered from childhood. But she had another, more vulnerable side. On one occasion I phoned her from the National Archives to let her know that I had been given permission by F.R. Scott's executor to read some of her early letters. She was so angry that I later said to her (after she had cooled down), "P.K. I can still feel your hot hooves on my forehead."

Nonetheless the biography continued to develop. The Page family and her good friends like Arlene Lampert, Rosemary Sullivan, Connie Rooke and Théa Gray co-operated in the information-gathering process. Every few months, for six years or so, I would leave my home in West Vancouver before 6 a.m. to catch the 7 a.m. ferry to Victoria in order to arrive at the Irwin home on 3260 Exeter Road for a full morning's work. P.K. would get up early and put the coffee on. We would then descend to Arthur's study in the basement and work there happily until called for lunch, and then continue on for a few hours in the afternoon. I would usually stay for three or four days, sometimes with P.K., sometimes with my niece who lived nearby.

My first task was to establish a chronology, as P.K. rarely remembered WHEN she had been WHERE, an essential for any biography. "That's your job," she would say. Eventually I was able to reconstruct a year-by-year record. The whole enterprise was greatly strengthened in 1999 when editor and textual scholar Zailig Pollock joined the project, initially to develop a chronology of Page's poems and short fiction, then a catalogue of her art, but ultimately to develop the scholarly apparatus for the larger study of her work as a whole. From my perspective, P.K.'s biography could not have been written without this essential scholarship.

The first third of the interviews went extremely well. P.K. enjoyed the biographical process of attempting to recall the past in response to my questions, and this led her to several new creative essays, including one on her father, and another on her mother taking tea with the Bates family in Calgary. Some of these essays brought her to new recognitions, others, I now think, were clouded by nostalgia for the idealized childhood that she wished to have had.

Arthur's death in August 1999, was a great blow. To a large degree Arthur had been P.K.'s emotional buffer against the world, offering unconditional love and common sense to the everyday travails of her working life as a poet. A little later, about halfway through the project, P.K. recognized that the process of having her biography written took up a great deal of her time—time she wanted for her own creative process. Some of these endeavors were fueled by the work we had been doing and led her to new autobiographical projects like *Hand Luggage, A Memoir in Verse* (2006) in which she recounts her life in her own accents. After P.K.'s death in 2010, I went back to the manuscript of her biography and re-wrote several sections of her life that she was, posthumously, making public in her obituary interview in *The Globe and Mail*.

She was, quite simply, a fine poet and an astonishingly gifted and generous woman. It was one of the great privileges of my life to have worked with her.

Solveig Adair

In my flesh, one bright section

The wax has melted/but the dream of flight/persists.
P.K. Page, "This Heavy Craft"

She wakes with feathers
in her mouth   her tongue heavy

on the street   old men
shuffle   their coats stretched too tight
for phantom wing buds

birds are everywhere
watching   the wires bending

the starlings reach with
their greedy hands and her beak
tries to break through her
real flesh   her cowardly lips

she remembers she hates
she loves the moment
we fall then we   rise and rise

her eyes close and she
can hear the sun close enough
to taste

she does not look up

My very brief story about P.K. Page

I want to have a conversation with P.K. Page. As an awkward teenager in a small rural community, P.K. Page wrote of a world both strange and somehow familiar and understandable. Her love of words, of impossible beautiful things that dull when they leave the mind and enter the pen, both inspired and discouraged me. I have rediscovered that magic, of words and writing, as I have aged and shared more of her experiences, more of an understanding of people who contain *"the area behind the eyes/where silent unrefractive whiteness lies."* I want to have a conversation with P.K. Page, but I've gradually realized that I've been having that conversation, year over year as I internalize and write to the images that she shared from her daring flights to the sun in the back of her creative mind.

Untitled

2005, PRIVATE COLLECTION, VICTORIA, BC. PEN AND COLOURED INKS.

This untitled sketch displays P.K.'s propensity for experimentation, as her scribblings suggest an automatic and gestural approach to composition, recalling her surrealist tendencies as a younger poet. The sketch resembles her Star Burst series, created in the early 2000s, done in gel ink, a relatively new medium at the time.

Rebecca Anne Banks

Untitled, 2005

"the morning dark thick with rain a day of shadows sunlight afternoon..."

rosebud blooms a touch of grace a touch of champagne to the rose was it a long war? how the day stopped we sit in the garden (amongst those that need barbed wire fences—radioland a new love, an old love) watch each other drink in loving eyes the beauty of enough hoping not to attract the guards the heralds of Berlin at the gate "surely he is not dead" my blonde soldier and virgin pink in the middle of the feast I look up (the colour of blond champagne the air of pink roses a full moon full sweet the air of roses drift...) and he was gone it is not dressage what the heart owns (I live for second chances although sometimes do not get them) you're different changed somehow he never said a word how the day goes the sounding church bells in the distance God knows the day brightens so for January trees...

Rebecca Anne Banks on P.K. Page

Reading P.K.'s beautiful verse, I was touched by the writing and the poem "The Metal and the Flower" which seemed to be the essence of sunlight in a crisp Canadian winter. This poem struck me, and I felt as if it could have been written by a former me from over fifty years ago. I was also struck by similar images appearing in my own untitled poem, written in the last year.

John Barton

A Son's Nineteen-Seventies Wardrobe

> *What the hand, dare seize the fire?*
>
> William Blake

Consider a new habit—classical
The skill she used to embroider my new
Jean jacket with roses, new leaves sprinkled
With runoff-blue, stitch-sized raindrops I knew

She took pains to make look real, knew she strew
Down vines buds yet to open, newly dropped
Petals around our patio renewed
In floss about the yoke, new deadheads lopped

But unrecorded, my youth a new crop
Of years she saw I'd not share, new threads
She bought me made newer still, sprays cupping
Shoulder blades newly squared, a blind spreading

Across my back, a newness I'd not see
When worn, nor the tiger she knew I'd free.

Illuminations

recasting P.K. Page's "After Reading
Albino Pheasants by Patrick Lane,"
with apologies to Arthur Rimbaud

At the bottom of the field
vagrant winter grasses clatter with sun
and I am lifted to a weightless world.

With eyes heavenwards and wind-rubbed skin peeled
back as thawed loam, I am coldly undone.
At the bottom of the field

uncaged birds—countless luminous calls hurled
deep into the ear where echoes, subterra, run
and I am lifted to a weightless world

of unchecked imaginings, inner maps about to yield
green-vowelled panoramas, blind flights begun
at the bottom of the field

of vision to far-off branches where, among half-curled
impatient leaves, uncertainties perch and stun
and I am lifted to a weightless world.

Inked thumbprint of cloud overhead as syllabics whorled.
Camouflage sloughed as feathers in rising abandon
at the bottom of the field
and I am lifted to a weightless world.

John Barton on P.K. Page

My first awareness of P.K. Page came via Gary Geddes. As my creative-writing teacher at the University of Alberta in 1977, he recommended that I hone my craft with her at UVic's Department of Creative Writing, where I enrolled in September 1978. Unbeknownst to Gary or to me, she had decided not to continue teaching, after only one year. Nevertheless, she was the lure that led me to a series of experiences and decisions that would make me the poet I am today.

My next encounter with her was, of course, through her work. In a UVic English class with Eli Mandel in 1980, he asked his students to write pastiches of two poems by a Canadian poet. I chose to write in the manner of P.K.'s "A Bark Drawing" (my poem is called "Hieroglyph"); and "Personal Landscape" ("Shared Landscape"). Through this act of mimicry, I learned a great deal about, and came to respect even more, her mastery of startling imagery, nimble line breaks, and, most importantly, the knack she had of knotting the thread of a poem through a progression of stimulating ideas.

It was only after I became the editor of *The Malahat Review* in 2004 that she and I would meet. Within a month of my return to Victoria after a twenty-year absence, she invited me to her home for a drink. It's then I came to know a little of the fully engaged mind and exacting woman behind the poems. I greatly benefited from her open support of me as editor and was very grateful when she would, on occasion, compliment me on an issue and in particular for the tribute issue that the magazine published in 2007 in honour of its founder, Robin Skelton. This meant a great deal to me, for she was also very candid about the fact that no love had been lost between them.

After I met P.K., I would read each of her new books, and her prolific output in diverse genres during the last years of her life made this both a delight and a challenge. I am a great fan of *Hand Luggage: A Memoir in Verse, The Filled Pen* (essays), and *Coal and Roses* (her second book of glosas, the poetic form that other Canadian poets, following her example, still write today). She continues to motivate me as a poet, both through her writing and by her example. Her engagement with ideas, verse forms, and the language itself sets a high standard.

Stephen T Berg

Wash of Sky After Sunset

> *...If I were to wash*
> *everything I own in mercury, would imagination*
> *run rampant in that suddenly silver world —*
> *free me from gravity, set me floating sky-*
> *ward — thistledown — permanently disburdened of my flesh?*
>
> P.K. Page, "After Reading *Albino Pheasants* by Patrick Lane"

It's not so much the stiffening flexion
or bone shrink under loosening flesh;

the so-called indignities of gravity
are not the heart's worry;

only let me look out over this grey bay
to the wash of sky after sunset

and smell the coming rains of winter,
let me welcome the slow-motion communion of forest

the colliding silences of songbirds
and the small black snake in the clipped grass,

guiding itself with its own signaling tongue,
toward the garden border's flowering thyme,

and I will rise like thistledown
in this silvery space

to float a few feet above my life,
my rampant past fully alive,

my future, a giant turtle
lumbering across the sand and

vanishing gracefully into the water,
which makes it harder and harder

not to love,
not to love everything here so much,

until there's nothing left but imagination
and this choir
           of anticipation.

Stephen T Berg on Reading P.K. Page

That first impression swept me up. It was summer. I was living in a small cabin in northern Alberta. With me was a copy of *15 Canadian Poets X2* (edited by Gary Geddes). I was reading *After Rain* and all these images formed and fell around me. Every line was a photograph, a *seeing* painting. I read on. Every poem was a gallery of some other world—strange and familiar. I longed to strike out on the journey she was on; weave this world together with that other, explore thresholds her poems seemed determined, destined to explore. Her imagination seemed a wild restless *spirit*—angular and hard it soared. As far as I know she isn't known as a poet of faith, but it's how I see her. Whether through the eyes of a stenographer or through the crystalline lens of snow or using rigged guys of rain, she reached always for an "other" place; rigorously, ardently, taking us with her. And I loved her for it.

Stephen Bett

Ken Cathers: the sum

(for Ken)

> *are we no more*
> *than skin*
> *sewn over desire*
> *unremembered flesh*
>> Ken Cathers, "the serial husband"

are we no more
than the sum of
the heart's frailest
missing pieces

than skin
if it comes to that
stretched cruel
& unusually thin

sewn over desire
which cuts a thousand ways
like lingchi's slow dice
dance across flesh

unremembered flesh
awake now to a descent
that lashes endless &
at odds with desire

Patrick Friesen: Dear Harmon

> *miles davis cupping his trumpet with a mute,*
> *a slippery sound, almost an escape, a caesura,*
> *hold, hold what? my breath, yes, but the watery*
> *applause in some club as well, bill evans having*

        Patrick Friesen, "mri"

miles davis cupping his trumpet with a mute,
dear harmon: that full round tone / &
sound bites / … can break / the heart
in / every / single / groove (doo bop bop

a slippery sound, almost an escape, a caesura,
a pause mid-zone or modal, like *so what* in the gut
nothing left … that / freakish, frenetic /
cartoonish / bop (we stack & cheat the poem

hold, *hold what? my breath, yes, but the watery*
choked 'n dented mute, hold yr breath in the mri, mr. b
yes, release molly b, & hold again for a count of ten
exquisite interjections / into blank space (spunk tube

applause in some club as well, bill evans having
flown the dupe, beel i'vaanz (en paree) weird & wired…
we had, by then / like totally / fused
(post-bop & cool blue u

Stephen Bett on P.K. Page

A brief description of *Broken Glosa: an alphabet book of post avant glosa*

My father took me to sit, age fifteen and starting out in poetry, at the feet of his friend P.K. Page, the doyenne of Canadian poetry, who later revived the "glosa" in Canada. My latest book, my twenty-fifth, in a sense brings it all back home. *Broken Glosa* takes the "glosa," a Renaissance Spanish Court form, and breaks it down to its contemporary essentials—fractured forms for fractured times—riffing on postmodernist and post-avant poets in ways that are as surprising and inventive as they are richly textured. This book surely plays out my lifetime in North American and British avant-gar-de poetry, taking the measure of seventy postmodernist poets.

And a note on P.K. Page

My father (President of the BC Conservative Party, a Red Tory himself and very pleased when I "got involved" as a member of the NDP in my early twenties) was a good friend of Arthur Irwin's, P.K.'s husband. P.K. and Arthur had just returned to Victoria from his posting as Canadian Ambassador in Mexico; they were living on Ripon Road, just a couple of blocks away from where I grew up. I had started writing poetry at fifteen and, through my dad, P.K. invited me to spend one Saturday afternoon in her living room, amongst all the pieces of art & artifacts she'd just brought back from Mexico. I sat very much at her feet, a quiet, shy kid, enthralled with her explanations of what it was (is!) to be a poet, and what her practice as a writer involved. I don't remember details (this was 1963, nearly sixty years ago now) but I do remember how very kind she was, and, especially, how genuinely encouraging. (The following year my dad introduced me to his fellow Yorkshireman, Robin Skelton, whom he had asked to spend an hour with me and my poetry—I was hardly a sixteen-year-year-old renegade Rimbaud, growing up in the Uplands, and Robin S told me I was using too many gerunds, which was certainly true!) In 1970 I became friends, in

Toronto, with the multi-media artist Vera Frenkel, again through my family. Vera gave me, quite literally, a note of introduction to Pat Martin Bates, P.K.'s very dear friend. These two formidable, but wonderful women— each named Pat—continued to encourage my work. Many decades later I learned they had been instrumental in ushering some of my early poems into the hands of a couple of poetry journal editors. How discrete they had been! And how incredibly kind!

By the Wave Rising, By the Wave Breaking

1961, Trent University, Peterborough, ON.
White ink on black paper.

Reproduced in *The Glass Air* (1985) under its original title "In the Wake," *By the Wave Rising, by the Wave Breaking* was created in Mexico during P.K.'s "dark" period. Unlike Brazil, where the rich, vibrant colours "pelted" the artist, Mexico appeared bathed in blackness: dark, mysterious, and mystical. P.K.'s bleak surroundings contributed to a period of spiritual, emotional, and creative tumult, during which she struggled to find her religious footing (through a failed introduction to Subud and eventual embrace of Sufism) and artistic identity (as she grappled with various media, including etching and painting, until finally finding egg tempera, a medium she found "supremely well suited to [her] temperament"). The expressive, gestural abstraction of this piece embodies the unsettling chaos of this period. In retrospect, she renamed the painting after the opening lines from her early imagist poem "The Crow" (1941), in which the titular avian harbinger of death stands like a "stiff / turn-the-eye-inward old man / in a cutaway" in the midst of the tumultuous world that surrounds it, implying the importance of such agitation to self growth and rebirth.

Barbara Black

Black Flag Warning: variation on a glosa

> *Night falls on the bright grass. The flowers blink out.*
> *Only the faintest afterglow remains—*
> *more like a phrase of music or a scent.*
> *A supra-sense is needed for the dark.*
>
> P.K. Page and Philip Stratford, "Garden, III"

> *First they take it away,*
> *for now the body belongs to the state.*
> *Then they open it*
> *to see what may have killed it*
>
> William Matthews, "My Father's Body"

I

We walk in the glitter of morning, dawn in our eyes,
sea flat as a canvas, stunned by beauty.
We forget. The sea's a concealment,
the slimmest surface atop a universe.
Not a painting, but a dying thing.
The day's diamonds, illusion.
Night falls on the bright grass. The flowers blink out.
Salmon succumb to heat-stressed hearts.
We can't fathom it. The strife and strain.
First they take it away.

II

All life is a perilous entanglement.
The earth is our body—the pain of speaking it.
Do we have to, like starfish, lose an arm?
Imagine limbs dissolving:
a self-dismemberment.
Part by part, orange and purple stars fade.
Only the faintest afterglow remains,

like a supernova collapsing in on itself.
"The end of the rotten line," they say,
for now the body belongs to the state.

III

The stench announces itself from miles away.
A black flag warning, a blast of awful
come to knock us off our feet.
When, these days, do we smell decaying flesh?
Is death a kind of beauty or just death?
No, the poetry of the sea, we insist, is
more like a phrase of music or a scent,
not this carcass humped like a boulder on the beach,
baleen frayed in a grimace.
Then they open it.

IV

There's nothing inside.
No guts, no organs, no cartilage, no bones.
No man huddled at a table with a candle stub.
No eggs, no young, no womb.
Not a spine, not a sinew, not a muscle, no fat.
Inside, what seems like nothing. Black.
A supra sense is needed for the dark.
Listen. Engines rev, ships pass, nets drag the bottom.
We squint in the dim and still we fail
to see what may have killed it.

Consider the Pangolin

carve into me with knives of light.
Something inside it reminds me of childhood—

Anne Carson, "The Glass Essay," in *Glass, Irony & God.*

I

I can't help thinking of the pangolin,
a toothless creature encased in armour.
The Creator made it so strange it is desired.
The pangolin looks inviolable but is not.
In China, people cut it into cubes for soup.
Its numbers dwindle. It wanders drylands
in the dark, thirsty for its soul, while eaters
spoon its body into their mouths.
If only it could pray don't
carve into me with knives of light.

II

Its Zimbabwean guardian leads it to water.
If there's nothing for its unfurling tongue,
the keeper carries it further in his arms.
In Guangdong a chef cuts the pangolin's throat.
Boils it to remove the scales. There are knives
hidden in a psalm. The terror that God doesn't care.
That supplication is sadness sung to ourselves.
The pangolin's tail drags a shape in the sand,
a question mark, with a gaping crook.
Something inside it reminds me of childhood—

Barbara Black on reading P.K. Page

The four lines by P.K. Page I borrowed for my glosa, "Black Flag Warning," are from Part II of "Garden," from the book, *And Once More Saw the Stars: Four Poems for Two Voices,* a lyrical and philosophical selection of rengas co-written by P.K. Page and Philip Stratford. I never met P.K. Page and by the time I discovered her work, she was already gone. But I met her in her words when I found Page's and Stratford's unique collection in a used bookstore and was astounded at the beautiful language, the notion of sharing a poem with another poet, and saddened at how the series ended. Their poems seemed to have fit all the universe and the human experience of it into a small but very poignant book.

Yvonne Blomer

What Tapestry

> *No one is moving now, the stillness is*
> *infinite. If I should make a break...*
> *take to my springy heels...? But nothing moves.*
> *The spinning world is stuck upon its poles*
>
> P.K. Page, "Arras"

Consider colour, radiance, the delicacy
of bones, of fingers; the hand that weaves.
Green, emerald, pine merge to grass
and leaf, shaded and lit by the sun;
how busy this scene:
poppies and ferns; buckets and coloured balls
like bubbled wishes; barking collie,
her voice peals, a bell on memory;
and a man sleeping, only his feet praise.
No one is moving now, the stillness is

of evening. All sound arrested
or sung through hollowed mouths.
Shadow crawls like coloured threads,
like caterpillars, their finest hairs bristling.
This scene: a tapestry—what hand,
fingers pinching colour, could make
such details hum; thrum of wasp
stitched in here and here.
Distance: call of siren or child shrieks
infinite. If I should make a break

it should search me out, the green eye
in the still scene. How to capture self here,
to spin and weave each new story
on the ancient fabric of soil and sun.
Meanwhile, one tree sparrow with hued

feathers, trilling song, stitches stillness,
calls the night in, to steal the day.
The moon, reflective and waning,
wants to be the eye. And I, excluded,
take to my springy heels...? But nothing moves.

Nothing comes or stays. Light, feathered,
evaporates. I think of you, P.K., your aging
body when the mind resolves to play on
as long as it can; and the eye
breathes in the day and the dusk's light.
You are like the one-eyed feather, pools
of colour and shimmering radiance. Immaculate
the dance, this song. You have woven
the finest tapestry; complete. Entered a knowing:
The spinning world is stuck upon its poles.

Monday's Mother

after a line from P.K. Page's "Isolationist"

My son, newborn, has slept late. The hours from conception
to this long-toothed day lays light across my face.
Unfaltering, that same light shimmies praise, passion
for my son, newborn and sleeping late. The hours from conception
to these two images: his new skin and mine, a deception
of light. Yet I'm immaculate and full of grace:
my son, newborn, sleeps late. While the hours from conception
to this long-toothed day lays light across my face.

Birthday Card for Daddie

1920, TRENT UNIVERSITY, PETERBOROUGH, ON.

Birthday Card for Daddie is part of P.K.'s juvenilia. The budding artist often formalized her artwork, which includes numerous illustrations of nursery rhymes, with borders and captions (typically written by her mother). This piece, created for her father on his birthday when P.K. was only four years old, displays a smiling, almost animated, figure wearing what appears to be a red cape. The careful attention P.K. has paid to keeping the watercolour inside the lines of her drawing (no small task at the tender age of four) is a testament to her raw talent.

Marilyn Bowering

I am a Poet's Cat— *

I sharpen my claws
on the alphabet

I butter my paws
and eat sentences raw

When I sleep on the bed
my toes are outspread

and I tread and I tread
through the books I have read

I am a poet's cat

I do more than rhyme
one line at a time

I hum and I purr
while editing verbs

reach the highest of notes
(so highbrow, my meow)

when I nibble on toast
and sometimes sardines

and baked langoustine

I can open bird cages
still turning through pages

(it doesn't take ages)

but I'm not always nice—
I do what I like
fill bathtubs with mice

Oh *burp* (pardon me!)—
they were up to my knees—

that is—
they gather in herds
and teach me new words

because
I am a poet's cat

* P.K.'s cats were the brothers *Prince Henry* and *Gringo*. She wrote ten books for children between 1989 and 2010. *A Grain of Sand* (2003), reflects on Blake's words: "To see a World in a Grain of Sand /And a Heaven in a Wild Flower/Hold Infinity in the palm of your hand/And Eternity in an hour."

Marilyn Bowering on P.K. Page

A Puff of Smoke

Early Years

I met P.K. Page in the early 1970s when I was a graduate student of Robin Skelton's. I don't now recall the particular circumstances, but I encountered her a number of times at poetry readings at UVIC. and elsewhere. She would always say hello and introduce me to whoever was with her. I met, that way, Floris McLaren, Anne Marriott and Doris Ferne—and began to have a sense of a living tradition of women poets so near at hand that no one appeared to know of them. They certainly weren't the poets giving the readings.

I travelled for the next few years, and when I returned to BC, I met up with P.K. again. This time we became friends, and she was an enthusiastic member of our Signal Hill (Victoria) poetry group—which included, among others, Jak English, Sandy Hutchison and Susan Musgrave. We ran poetry readings and published, distributed, and sold broadsides in the city. In July 1977 I left the country to live in Scotland and it is from that period I have my earliest letters from her.

In one of these, she mentions our Signal Hill group and the latest broadsides, and: "I was working with Arlene [Lampert] this summer on the cassettes project which I got involved in at the last League meeting. [The 'cassette project' was the League's living archive initiative.] We have found an expert to do the taping who is also knowledgeable about and interested in poetry. In fact, we have found everything but the money—and that, we hope will be forthcoming."

Plus ça change … !

P.K. liked poetry better when she "wasn't sure what it meant." She didn't like to define it and refused to explain her own work. When pushed to public statement she drew on T.S. Eliot's words* (this is her gloss on them) "that the meaning of the poem is provided to keep the mind busy while the poem goes on with its work—like the bone thrown to the dog by the robber so he can get on with *his* work."

She was pinned down another time and commented, "I must admit to a liking for the words of Dr. Thomas Fuller, a seventeenth-century physician who said, "Poetry is a dangerous honey. I advise thee only to taste it with the Tip of thy finger and not to live upon it. If thou do'st, it will disorder thy head and give thee dangerous Vertigo's."

You could say that her recipe for poetry was:

Honey
and Vertigo
and a Bone for the Dog.

P.K. was "light-hearted, quick-witted and surreal"—words she used to describe the people of Brazil she so admired. She delighted in these qualities in others—like the poet and Old Norse translator George Johnston who brought a dripping honeycomb from his Quebec hives in his suitcase as a present for her. She ends the letter to me I have mentioned, by referring to some Highland gleanings I had sent her: "Thank you for the feather and the wool. Nothing can be enclosed in this [airmail letter] but a puff of smoke. And love."

* T.S. Eliot — *The Use of Poetry and the Use of Criticism* [Harvard University Press, 1933].

Votive Tablet

1972, PRIVATE COLLECTION, OTTAWA, ON. EGG TEMPERA ON GOLD LEAF.

Votive Tablet prominently displays, through its various geometric shapes and patterns, the "circling of the square": a common concept in Eastern art, symbolizing the transformation of "earth into heaven" (Page, "Darkinbad" 40). As its title suggests, this piece serves as a spiritual offering, a means of prayer through artistic praxis for P.K., who was deeply committed to Sufism at this point in her career.

Kate Braid

Tree Song

> *Naked trees extend their complicated praise*
> *branches sway, in*
>   *a sort of unison*
>   *not agreed upon*
>   *each their own way*

   John Terpstra, "Naked Trees"

May I be forgiven, may I forgive
myself this endless search for someone, some
thing to explain, give me the reason we're here
and what lies after and if there's a plan
(or even better) Planner—if I could only
know for sure (just once? a deal? I'll stay
right here, you whisper in my ear, The Answer...)
while all around me animals carry on
regardless. Plants and insects don't bother counting days
and naked trees extend their complicated praise.

Why them? How can they praise and not await
reward? Who do they praise? What? How
can they stand there, splendid, and not ask why or if
there is a goal? At least a prize
for the very best? Do they dream of after-death or fear
old age or insects or men with saws? Can it matter
that underneath the soil they're all in touch—
what one knows, all know instantly in a deciduous,
coniferous vocabulary that whispers a grace, as all around
branches sway in a sort of unison.

Perhaps I should sit and watch, listen
for a while, to the shushing of trees,
peace in one place, a salute to sky
and no complaints unless you count the crack
of the final fall and what do they see then?
Is there mortal terror? Or a welcome to the stones
they shall now lie upon, the bed from which to nourish
other trees? If we die childless are we
forgotten? Is heaven a tonic
not agreed upon?

Some say there's nothing to be frightened of,
there's God or gods or goddesses or not, to take me "home"
or not. I'll find out soon enough, that's sure.
Perhaps this is my fascination with birds
who fly above, rest lightly on each moment,
small prayers to the beginning and end of day.
And after all, how can it matter that I get the story right
or wrong? When it comes to living—life and death—
each being sings a sort of roundelay,
each their own way.

Mumbai

for H.B. and with thanks to P.K.

I hear a rustle of leaves and wake
to see the curly head of a dark-skinned man
visible through greenery around the window
beside my bed.

I scream, *Get out!* over and over
my voice gravel, *Get out!*
And that's when I wake
and there is no man.
There is no window beside my bed,
no greenery.

But for days the dream lingers like a stuck tune.
The face was not malevolent, not evil, not even angry.
It merely watched, curious

as if someone from another world had laid his head
against the thin wall of this labyrinth called *home*
and could see me here, on the other side,
and I could see his seeing.

Did I tell you his face showed no anger?

On that night, somewhere, did a dark-skinned man dream
of a pale-skinned woman, afraid? I ask myself—
what if I had waited just one moment before I screamed?
What if I had looked back, curious? Said hello?

What if he had spoken, had something important to say?
What if I had listened?

Kate Braid on P.K. Page

Patricia Kathleen Page

> *prepare*
> *for what you have dreamed to burn and be burned*
>
> P.K. Page, "Preparation"

Ah, dear P.K.
your courage
dazzles me.

Dear P.K.
your courage
terrifies me.

To face unknown forces,
to evoke the gods,
dare fire, dare
to be burned and then
to pick up the pen
and write about it.

I got to know P.K. when Sandy Shreve and I were looking for someone to write the Introduction to our upcoming anthology, *In Fine Form*, on Canadian form poetry. Who better than the only woman we knew who could actually write in metre and make it seem conversational, who'd recently introduced glosas to the Canadian poetry world? Marilyn Bowering introduced us, and P.K. graciously agreed to the Introduction. Further, she came to our launch of the book in Victoria, which is where we first met in person. She invited us to visit and from then on, every few months I took the ferry from Vancouver, where I lived, to spend an afternoon with P.K. in Victoria, talking and drinking wine. P.K. rapidly became a mentor to me. Apart from the splendour of her poetry, her grace, her intelligence, her sense of humour and yes, her delicious love of gossip, I was awed by her spiritual courage. Here was a woman who fearlessly searched beyond this reality, not just accepting but seeking to explore other realities, which she was certain were there. P.K. gave me enormous courage as a poet and as a woman, and I will be forever grateful. I deeply miss her.

Terry Ann Carter

Room

after P.K. Page, "Deaf-Mute in the Pear Tree"

And how did the apple become red
and round, and how did the oil
and vinegar fill their small jars.

The fork and knife—how did they
find their way to this table. And the bowl
of bananas created by the blind potter.

Poetry books line the sill, carried
in a woven basket and placed
one by one, where a view of the mountain

fills every frame. How I trekked to northern
Cambodia to sit in the temples of Angkor Wat
a volume of P.K. Page in a backpack.

Frangipani petals still folded into a binding.
And the small counter with salts and seasonings
a fan above the stove. How I love this room

the way P.K.'s deaf mute loves his wife
looking down from a pear tree. The air
filled with kisses. Kisses.

Terry Ann Carter on P.K. Page

I brought three volumes of poetry with me when I went to Cambodia to work with the Tabitha Foundation, in the early 2000s. One by P.K. Page, one by Lorna Crozier, and one by Jane Hirschfield. I needed "the women" to help me keep grounded when I travelled throughout this stricken country. I needed poets' eyes to remind me to constantly look for beauty in the torn places. The poem about the deaf mute always filled me with joy. I loved reading it over and over again.

Lorna Crozier

P.K.

She saw two moons in the prairie sky.
As a girl, when asked if she were cursed
with seeing double, she replied,
Oh, no. If I were, then I'd see four.

In countries with no cold,
snow from her childhood
fell circular and soft
in the glass globe of her inner eye,
dressing the blossoms as if they were brides.

Her only child was the child she dreamed
and folded in a box like a scarf
woven out of rain. You could say
she neglected God and his angels,
though the invisible made sense
in all her senses. Heaven she found

in the gaze of a glorious macaw
with the face of Groucho Marx,
and once, with her calm uncanny eye,
as a marmoset in a rage sunk its teeth
in the flesh just above her wrist,
she noticed its fingers
were the stems of violets.

In a poem, at the moment of death,
the poet asked, *What is the correct procedure?*
Cut the umbilicus, they said.
Now she has cut it and risen from the page.
Beneath her, the Earth is the size of a plum
and the blue of a plum when it is ripe with morning.

Is the body still a body, she wonders,
if it is drifting so high? How, then, to prepare it?
Wash it in sacred water is her own reply.
Dress it in silk for the wedding.

Lorna Crozier on P.K. Page

One evening, out of the blue, P.K. gave me a plastic grocery bag after we'd finished a reading together in Victoria. Inside were two leather belts with huge, round silver buckles. One belt was black, the other white. The size was adjustable. She said, "I bought these decades ago in Brazil, and I don't wear them anymore because I've given up in my old age on belts. If anyone can wear them, I thought, it's Lorna." Well, I did wear them, that is, for many years. The big flashy buckles were similar to those worn by rodeo cowboys or wrestling champs. When I was nervous about a reading or presentation, they gave me confidence. Her gesture was such a generous, female thing to do. I'll soon have to pass them on to someone else, a younger woman poet who I think will love them as much as I did, someone whose shyness and fear might be overcome by that hefty weight around the waist, that cinched hug, passed on from one generation to the next.

Babe's View of Planet Earth

1994, PRIVATE COLLECTION. OIL STICK.

"Babe" is a nickname for the narrator and protagonist of P.K.'s novella *Unless the Eye Catch Fire...* in which the earth is gradually being destroyed by the gradual heating up of its interior. Joy Coghill adapted the novella as a dramatic monologue and performed it as part of a festival in honour of the Commonwealth Games in Victoria in 1994.

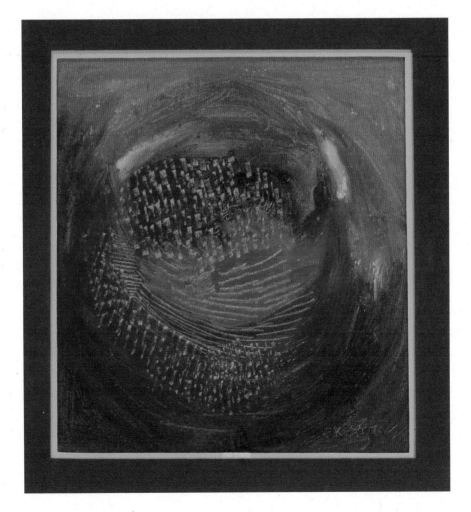

Wendy Donawa

On Reading P.K. Page's "Stories of Snow"

Night fading, unseasonal snowdrifts
lifting river mist, cliffs dissolved.
Leaving seemed
a dream
of departure.

Next dawn, waking
to a pale ceiling awash
with absence of everything but morning light.

Strange then to encounter P. K.'s poem:
snow light falling white
among the swans, drift of their down, and
men in a colourless landscape
who dream their way to death.

Still, I bought these white freesias,
star-bright,
to conjure your face.

Aubade

with lines from P.K. Page's "The Last Time"

In that long twilight before sun-up
grey light seeps through blinds,
stripes my drams where
lost boys wander the corridors,
surface through light and shadow
until they fade.

Everything aches.
This friendly body, my good animal,
now slow to my bidding,
hatches mutinous cells and clamours for sleep.
Shall I lie with my nails painted, my hair curled
awaiting my beloved, as of old?
Of that coltish girl no remnant,
not even in the deepest mirror.
When did I start to be old?

The sun
stamps its bright bar code on the wall,
and I turn to you
and our late love in these flannel sheets.

What we say goodbye to
—the romp and flex of salad days,
supple muscles heedless of the night—
gives lustre to all that our stitched bodies
have scavenged from a shattered world,
weight of loss and loving.

Somehow catastrophe's patina
glosses our *now* of pleasure:
raku still glowing from the kiln.
        It's not late yet.

Wendy Donawa on P.K. Page's Influence

I have been entranced by the elegant sensuousness and exquisite craft of P.K.'s poetry ever since I discovered her on my return to Canada. In particular, I was moved by her 2009 glosa collection, *Coal and Roses*; in her nineties, she wrote one of the most tenderly erotic poems I've read ("Your Slightest Look," in case you want to check it out). For anyone heading glumly into the so-called golden years, it's very encouraging!

Margaret Slavin Dyment

Learn to Write

> *and, if our future here is unconfirmed,*
> *and we are on probation, maybe I*
> *must change my tune, my scale even, and try*
> *some left-brain reasoned thinking, learn to write*
>
> P. K. Page, "Address at Simon Fraser, 1990"

"I am not well," you say. "It's been a bad year,"
and I see time pass over you, this change.
"I'm eighty-six—what can we expect?"—I echo you:
what can we, as we wind back down…
"Your hip is better now?" That elegant black cane
is gone, your metamorphosis affirmed,
your beauty melting in the stress of shortened
 breath. "It tires me," you say steadily.
"We need our breath," I say. You catch at yours, infirm
and, if our future here is unconfirmed,

what else is new? He lived so long, but you
and most of us find eighty-six a turning point
or eighty-seven. The speaker shows us
photos of your childhood, your first poem
—your voice was crystalline, already there,
as you decided: "More than anything I
want to be a good poet." But not political,
even then. By choice. As now. Your young heart
entered its correlative, learned metaphors must cry
and we are on probation, maybe I

commit a comma splice to implement
this glosa rule; its punctuation caught me unaware
but maybe we are on probation, true, uncertain how to write
and also take the time to traipse the planet while we're here,
this one life we know, with bombs and sniper fire
and children homeless on the street—how can we justify

making glosa, turning off the phone,
inventing stories, images of fire, rain and snow?
The world burns, literally—yet still may be that I
must change my tune, my scale even, and try

what love can do, as Quakers say, picketing outside
in rain and cold and snow and sun, with simple words:
A million dead. Albright says it's worth the price.
End sanctions now. And: Need, not Greed.
"It's time we met," you'd said, and so we did, downtown;
then later over tea you read a villanelle; I learned to cite
more right-brain intuition, foolishness and dream
and trust that opening behind the eye-caught-fire; peacock
iris widens now with hope I'll put to flight
some left-brain reasoned thinking, learn to write!

Margaret Slavin Dyment on P.K. Page

When I lived in Victoria, BC, 1990–2000, I taught creative writing from my home. A phone call came in from P.K. Page out of the blue: "Isn't it time that we met?" This led to several visits together and a warm sense of being welcomed into the writing community of Victoria. After my move back to Peterborough, Ontario, when Trent University held a *festschrift* to celebrate P.K.'s writing and visual art, I attended, bringing with me quatrains from Page's work that had spoken to me. As the event unfolded, so did the glosa, one of which is included here.

Patrick Friesen

#59

dreams have been leaping
between now and then

and then goes both ways
if you think of it

an elegant boatman
poling the raft

like that old poet
impossibly tall with her white swan cane

and I never dreamed her
though she was in my dreams

who was she?
from some beautiful world

and now and now
well that was then

and it will be then
when the raft rides ashore

those swans gliding
away

Patrick Friesen with a story about P.K. Page

In 2005 I told P.K. I was going to Lisbon for a month. She said, very seriously, "Oh, you have to buy another flight to Granada to see the Alhambra; I've always wanted to visit it, but now I never will." So, I did as requested and flew from Lisbon to Granada. I arrived near midnight and decided I had to give P.K. a brief description of what I could see. The owner of the B&B asked me to follow him up two floors to the roof of the building. On the roof was a fantastic garden, and right in front of me, across the Darro River, the lights of the Alhambra. I phoned P.K. and told her what I saw. Because of that visit I discovered the Generalife Gardens behind the palaces of the Alhambra, gardens with more than 1000 different water sounds according to a British engineer. And I met Simon Andrewes, a Brit writer living in Granada, who knew a lot about Lorca and took me for a full day's tour of Lorca's last week, ending up at the possible burial site in the hills outside the city. All because of P.K.

Catherine Graham

Chthonic

after Dorothy Molloy, "The Woman and the Hill"

The lilacs have risen to solo in the corner orchestra of greens.
Purple odours permeate the branched alveoli of my lungs.
I slip through the briars, listen to wind shaking the canopy, stand
in place till I'm pulled through the port of entry.

I fight. Play possum. But my wit leaks as lilacs rust
from bone ivory. Death seeps. I hold
my breath to tease the light they say is coming,
but like *the trees I* darken *the forest.*

You must find the hidden passage inside the earth's purse.
Chewing worms. Burrowing owls! Nothing is still,
not even my mind turning to brain, a field in fallow. The earth
slides over my face. I see the exchange that's happening—

a dead mother wants out. Her red hair rises with the wings
of insects, and I sink further than *the lair of the fox.*

The Bullied

after Dorothy Molloy, "Freed Spirit"

When I play invisible, the boy
sneers. I look away
and he's still looking.
His gathering of buddies
mock me with their yawn-traps.
You must learn how to look
and look back.

Can they see me now
when I press against the red brick wall
as they play Planet of the Apes?
I'm the lost thought inside the ocean
in Mrs. Easy's atlas.
How I'm gyred through the ether
is how God made me.

We are all icebergs to turn
green inside. Clouds hang
at half-mast. Another mother
is dying. The sun screams
yellow until the ding
of the recess bell. I fall in line.
Can they see in this stalk of wild fennel,

the twinkle of my silver buckle?
Big feet, they snigger.
I feel dot small. The crayon wave
on my paper rides the hair of water.
The scent of chalk is not home.
You pay a price when the cat's got your tongue.
Fire in the face, the cinder *and spark.*

Catherine on her poems and P.K. Page

The poems "Chthonic" and "The Bullied" are from my fifth poetry collection, *Her Red Hair Rises with the Wings of Insects*. This is a collection of deconstructed glosas that was originally a manuscript of glosas. Each cabeza (the four lines chosen from another poet's work) came from the work of Dorothy Molloy, an Irish poet who died ten days before her first book appeared with Faber and Faber. P.K. Page's masterful work with the glosa inspired me to try my hand at the form and I am grateful for her inspiration. Page and Molloy became my spirit mentors during the writing of this book. *Her Red Hair Rises with the Wings of Insects* is dedicated to their memories.

A Grey Goose Afternoon in Victoria

Our realtor happens to be P.K. Page's grandson, Arthur Irwin (a fantastic realtor by the way!) and when my partner John and I were planning a trip to BC a few years ago John, unbeknownst to me, had made arrangements through Arthur for us to meet my literary hero, P.K. Page. I was very nervous when I found out about the invitation to visit her home one Sunday afternoon. I'd heard her read before, and had been a fan of her work for years, but had never met her. Next thing I knew, there she was at the top of the stairs warmly inviting us into her home. Arthur had mentioned she liked Grey Goose Vodka, so after presenting her with a bottle we proceeded to get tipsy with P.K.! The lovely afternoon went by so fast. After she signed my books, I gave her a copy of my poetry collection, *Pupa* . "Thank you," she said and then she looked me in the eye. "You know, I might not like it." A week later she sent me an email to let me know how much she liked my work. I was thrilled.

Planet Earth

1964, PRIVATE COLLECTION. GOLD LEAF AND EGG TEMPERA.

In Mexico, P.K. created a series of paintings of large globes, including *Planet Earth*. The titles of these globe paintings, including *To be Lost in the Incandescence of a Personal Universe,* and their application of gold leaf—traditionally used in religious art to evoke spiritual or mystical significance—indicate a reflection on the spiritual essence of the cosmos. Her poem of the same name, written many years later, affirms the preciousness of this medium, declaring "it has to be made bright, the skin of this planet."

Heidi Greco and Sandy Shreve

In Praise of Planet Earth

a renga after P.K. Page's "Planet Earth"

It has to be loved
with flowers and birds, praising
holy surfaces—
polished as coloured pebbles
hidden in rivers and streams.

It has to be washed,
smoothed with water and brightness,
pressed into metres of stars
the way a mother attends,
coaxing within and above.

It has to be loved,
newly shined until the skin
of this planet, its
trees and grasses and mosses
are singing their hosannas.

We must love it till
it is burnished to blisses
and blessings. The great
sea and all its creatures made
beloved, bright and holy.

It must be showered
and rubbed by hands day and night:
the flower-blue lake
with its grey sky overhead,
Archangels will polish it,

Seraphim paint it
with sheets of pale blue rain. Then
the green of this world
will blazon forth and the sea,
protean and pleated, move

our hands to draw it
with pencils and brushes; keep
moving and smoothing—
the way two joined hands are washed.
This shining planet,

her sun like gold—such
an O!—has to be stroked like
a lover knowing
the way—and celebrated,
her cresses spread out, in leaf.

Heidi Greco and Sandy Shreve
on their poem and P.K. Page

A few years ago, we were invited to an event honouring P.K. Page. To celebrate, we composed a renga (yes, we each sent lines back and forth via emails to create the piece), but to add to the challenge, we restricted ourselves to words P.K. had used in her poem, "Planet Earth" which she'd devised 'after Neruda' and his wonderful Ironing poem.

It took a while, but we managed to use the words in Page's poem, rearranging them as carefully as if we were ironing them.

Janel Halenko

This Space

after P.K. Page, "Another Space"

wild sand
sparkles like glittered gold
a kaleidoscope
of beauty repeated
we spin this shape from a distance
popular cylinders
on the edge of liquid

looking at that moon
it means well
gales and tides alike move at incomprehensible speeds
words unravelling half as quickly
twice as perplexing
proposed this space
on this axis
cannot be determined—
is set
if only in dream

You merge: a shadow of a different shape
while we spin on our rim
our pull steady
our height teasing
the moon
choosing presence
we make shapes to represent this freedom

the air weaving the web of itself
the serendipitous figures that clouds form
are we creating?
we join hands horizontally
still spinning
why,
are we always spinning
on this hinge?

Janel Halenko on reading P.K. Page

"This Space" is a direct response to P.K. Page's poem "Another Space" and is my interpretation of the poem. I have revisited this poem almost daily for the past month now and have deduced that it may be an exploration of human ambivalence toward nature and the ceaseless necessity to label and justify all actions and events.

Hand

1963, Trent University, Peterborough, ON. Ink.

P.K. created this drawing towards the end of her time in Mexico. Like a number of the works of the period it blurs the boundary between abstraction and representation. In its overall effect it clearly represents a hand but its swirling details are anything but hand-like and suggest that the hand is at any moment about to dissolve into chaos. At this time P.K. was exploring various forms of mysticism culminating in Sufism. There may be a reference here to the Muslim symbol of the Hand of Fatima, about which P.K. wrote; and the interlocking triangles at the bottom of the page may be a representation of the crossed *dharmodaya*, a Hindu symbol of creation. The symbol also sometimes occurs in Sufism.

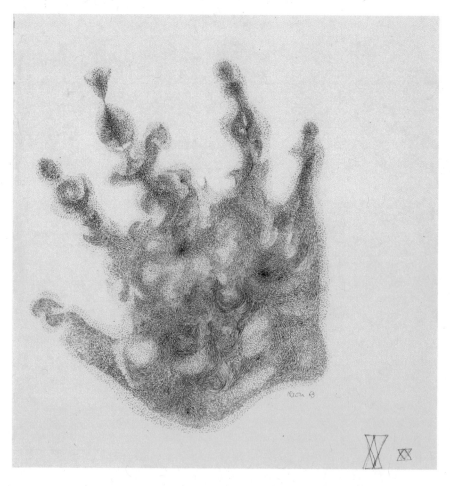

Marvyne Jenoff

It's There

Doctors know it's there, some artists, too:
the bump at the base of the thumb
with its little cheek.

Knitters discover it, once we advance
to the four-needle knitting-in-the-round stage,
past socks, to gloves.

A firm ribbed cuff to warm the wrist
and then that tricky, satisfying part:
a fifth needle picks up stitches for a gusset;
each new row diagonally grows to protect
the jutting bone that branches sideways
like a winter tree.

The glove is easy to complete:
repeat in mirror image for its mate
and find another friend to knit for,
though it's not the friend's need
but the knitter's.

Glove after glorious glove she makes
for the sake of making them:
a series of self-portraits are they,
not ironic drawings
nor oil paintings preserving age after age,
but portraits that fond repetition spawns.

The Warmth Giver lives long
in the practice of her ancient art,
embraces new approaches;
unimagined yarns excite her mind,
while all we knitters come at last to this:
the odd stitch disappears,
through our astonished fingers the yarn slips,

thumbs stumble and protest in pain.
To soothe it, doctors say,
use ice.

Marvyne Jenoff on P.K. Page

Though I knew Pat (P.K.) mainly at a distance I always admired her genuineness and graciousness. Her work as a visual artist showed that a poet needn't be restricted to one field of creativity. I have followed her lead with a career in the visual arts, as well.

Eve Joseph

All Morning...

All morning wind has banked a grey wing over the city. On the prairies it is a cry in a stairwell, a foundling. On the coast, a sail of salt. An ancient highway between Hakuba and Otari. As much as anything, we want to know that when the boat capsizes we can hang on. We will not necessarily understand. Take Nijinsky's last journal entry for instance: *My little girl singing ah ah ah… she wants to say everything is not horror, but joy.* When you died, wind shook the windows. You, who conjured Charlemagne, left us here unarmed and wildly unprepared.

Flowers and Phone

1958, PRIVATE COLLECTION, YELLOWKNIFE, NWT. FELT PEN AND GOUACHE.

Flowers and Phone displays P.K.'s transition from sketching in black felt pen to her incorporation of colourful gouache alongside this earlier medium. The juxtaposition of bright colourful paint against the dark pen in this particular piece also highlights the thematic tensions of her subject: between the organic and inorganic, between the old and new, and even between the metal (telephone) and the flower—a dynamic prominently explored in her most recent collection of the same title. As others have noted (Godard, Ballantyne), *Flowers and Phone* also hints at the poet's "communicational impasse" brought on by the overwhelming "sensory delight" of Brazil and its foreign tongue.

Beth Kope

Love Letter

P.K., give me your goldfish pond, the gold that burns within,
for me to find my swirling reflection.

P.K., give me your sandals, the ones you wore into the backyard
when peacocks stalked and strutted, rattled rattan tails.

P.K., give me your bracelet, heavy silver gripped and bonded on your wrist,
weighing your writing hand down with shimmer and flash.

Give me the pear tree you watched, the finches you observed.
The salt mine.

Give me the Chinese boxes that wear their lacquer like lipstick
that hinge and nestle.

P.K., I want your dreams from the dark of your sleep:
brocade curtains drawn, glycerined-green leaves, figures forever waiting.

I want to follow you into a Mexican fever, full of golden dust, a rain
of golden sun pouring onto entangled lobelias

I want your scent, a perfume of sea and longing,
of peony and magnolia, of hibiscus *in a froth and buzz*

tethered
to your glass air.

I want the cards you hold in your hand, and
the disguise you wear like a shawl.

Leila Kulpas

Transformations

I'm beginning to know the loveliness
of the things in the old house.
Indigenous carvings, vases,
masks in the stairwell, a Persian relief.
Objects discovered and treasured
by your father.

As I gaze at them,
their shapes, hues, planes and lines
emerge into wholeness,
increasingly complex,
and lovely.

When the house is empty,
they must ache for the caress of eyes,
your voice to tongue their fragmented stories.
Or perhaps, like Mexican street children
proffering gardenias in funnels of newspaper
at the edge of a fiesta,
they're glad of the gloom.

You say they're like parts of you,
and your beauty, like theirs,
continues to emerge
from the shadows.

Patrick Lane

The Measure

for P.K. Page

What is the measure then, the magpie in the field
watching over death, the dog's eyes hard as marbles
breath still frozen to his lips? This quiet repose,

the land having given up the battle against sleep,
the voices crying out beneath the snow.
It is the cold spear of the wind piercing me

that makes me sing of this, the hunger in your eyes.
It is the room of your retreat,
the strain in the hand when it reaches out to touch

the dried and frozen flowers brittle in their vase,
the strain when the mind desires praise,
the music as of soldiers wandering among their dead

or the poor dreaming of wandering as they break
their mouths open to sing as prisoners sing.
Or soldiers marching toward their devotions

or the poor marching or the rich in their dark
rooms of commerce saying this is finally the answer,
this will allow us the right to be and be. To be

anything. In the field the rare
stalks of grass stick stiffly into the air.
The poor, the broken people, the endless suffering

we are heir to, given to desire and gaining little.
To find the arms across the breast and fly
into ourselves. That painless darkness. Or stand

in the field with nothing everywhere and watch
the first flakes falling and pray for the deliverance
of the grass, a dog's death in the snow? Look

there. Stark as charred bone
a magpie stuns his tongue against the wind
and the wind steals the rattle of his cry.

Lorna Crozier

A story of P.K. Page and Patrick Lane

My husband, Patrick Lane, had more social encounters with P.K. than I did. One of the stories he liked to tell was about the two of them clowning around at a literary party in Toronto. I know some might not attach the word "clowning" with P.K. but she had a wicked sense of humour and enjoyed a good time. For some reason, Patrick and P.K. had been bragging about how they'd be okay if they got falling-down-drunk because they'd both learned how to land without injuring themselves. Their tutors were their friends, different ones of course, who happened to be stage actors. P.K. and Patrick challenged each another to prove their expertise, and to the surprise of the other revellers in the room, the two poets, neither of them young, started falling. Again and again. I wasn't there, but I can hear them laughing and I bet they teased and goaded until they complicated their game, daring one another to fall with a drink in hand without spilling a drop.

Fowl Yard

1959, PRIVATE COLLECTION. FELT PEN AND STENCIL.

While the Irwins were staying with a wealthy farmer in Brazil, P.K. crafted stencils of their hens. Later, she used the stencils in several works, including *Fowl Yard*, one of the few iconic abstractions in her oeuvre. The drawing has a surprising pop art aesthetic—its boldly-rendered subject having a modish place in 1950s kitchen décor—given that the piece pre-dates the height of the pop art movement in the 1960s.

Christopher Levenson

Macaw

in memoriam P.K. Page

Fitting that in Brazil
you had a pet macaw,
for such an alert
brilliantly mocking
creature becomes you.

Fine feathers, a finer
intellect, and a bright,
sharply observing eye.
They too live long
and have long memories.
Their purple and gold
emblazons the foliage.
They communicate
exactly.

So, incandescent, you
fly up, to guide us through,
ablaze with words,
inquisitive, elegant.
How could we not believe
you would be there forever?

But now the bird has flown.

Dvora Levin

Entitled Fragments

> *Like Dante's vision of the nether hell*
> *men struggle with the bright cold fires of salt,*
> *locked in the black inferno of the rock:*
> *the filer here, not innocence but guilt.*

> P.K. Page, "Photos of a Salt Mine"*

A Single Traveller with no maps,
every route a mystery, her Filled Pen
records Ten As Twenty, so many imaginings
to stuff into her Hand Luggage, store
inside a Hidden Room, always at the ready.

She travels her own unique journey.
To escape The Evening Dance of the Grey Flies,
she swims underwater, a Leviathan In A Pool,
dares to share *Dante's vision of the nether hell.*

Coal And Roses, The Metal And The Flower,
she sojourns with the mystics of the paradox.
As *men struggle with the bright cold fires of salt,*
her painter eyes catch fire hot enough to melt
The Glass Air of Planet Earth.

Traveling beyond the optical, beyond
the written word, she opens the vanishing point
locked in the black inferno of the rock
to cry her exquisite Ah, of The Golden Lilies.

She *filters here* (and not here), *not innocence,*
and not *guilt,* to illuminate the Hologram
to Kaleidoscope the twin circles of her conjurer's art.

Now fabled, A Grain of Sand in a Flask Of Sea Water,
she travels the Cosmologies, far beyond
her Sky Tree's stars, leaving us to forage
in the flickering fragments of P.K. Page.

+Capitalized phrases are book/poem titles.
*Quote from "Photos of a Salt Mine" (1946)

Dvora Levin on P.K. Page

On reading P.K. Page's poetry, I found reflections of her deepening sense of the mystical before I learned she had studied Sufism extensively, believing in the one and the oneness of everything.

Dan MacIsaac

Page: Esprit

Eye for the ordinary,
ear for the ornate,

saying the least
with the most brio.

Eye for the honest,
ear for the opulent,

revealing the most
and the least,

her fine esprit
glistering.

Diplomacy of verse
she dabbled in

then chose
resplendence.

Poems of pier glass
shimmering light

that turned
the flower's face,

lyrics tuned
to the true pitch,

the timbre
of stars spiralling

in the grand
sound box

of space.

Remembrance of a Reading

In the '80s, I attended a reading by P.K. Page in the big Mac 144 room at the University of Victoria. She began with richly embroidered poetry, weaving an intricate arras of blooms and brash peacocks. Rapt, her audience entered that tapestry. Then she read "Stefan." The poem was startling in its direct simplicity, its brevity, its insight. The poet reported what eleven-year-old Stefan observed about a baby, "When he thinks it must be pure thought/ because he hasn't any words yet." Surprised by this innocent insight, the poem's grownups, "looked at the baby again." When the author finished reciting her piece, a choral Ah! filled the auditorium. Each of us looked anew with the mind's clear eye at the infant. Ordinary became extraordinary, an ideal conjured by image and sound. There was an astounding echo effect: looking and listening both inside and outside the poem. That evening in Mac 144, P.K. Page called on us to perceive, to wonder, to look yet once more. Later, she would include "Stefan" in her brilliant anthology of short Canadian verse, *To Say the Least: Canadian Poets from A to Z*. Among that jeweler's collection of prize gems, those fine poetic equivalents of amber, jet and jade, "Stefan" gleams like an ice diamond.

Alice Major

Glosa: Parting

but there is more
what falls apart is held together
each
atom aligned

       P. K. Page, "For Mstislav Rostropovich with Love"

Second childhood.
His brain tearing
its figured lace, forgetting
the tale that held it all together.
She dreads the odor of
      this ward on the second floor.
Sometimes death would be the easier
of partings. Sore, yes,
      but not this sore.
But there is more.

Always more. She had never cared
for babies. Smelly nappies
drooping from safety pins.
Tedium's ether—
the looking after
and after, whatever weather
whirled the world skyward.
She dreaded the harness,
to be told forever
what falls apart must be held together.

Now his mind falls
apart, eighty
years and words
a repetitious dust.
Over and
over she tried to teach
now you do
this, this, this. Fastening moments
each
to each.

And now the parting every time
she leaves the ward—
his small, heartbreaking wave
to the closing door
of the elevator.
　　His life confined
and her leaving. Rupture
of what had been
so long entwined,
atoms aligned.

Alice Major on P.K. Page

Why would you say that?

P.K. Page was being interviewed by Peter Gzowski on his Morningside ra-
dio program. It was April, 1991. I was still working on my first book of
poetry, listening to this accomplished woman who had won a GG award
in her mid-thirties read "Lily on a Patio." Then, after the interviewer's ad-
miring comments, she said something like "When I wrote this, I thought it
might be the last poem I'd ever write."

And Peter Gzowksi didn't ask the question that was screaming in my
brain: "Why would you say that?"

Why would any poet ever say that? It terrified me—the idea that
poetry might up and leave. I was already in my early forties; maybe I just
wouldn't have the time to create a body of work of any significance at all.

I've thought about her remark many times in the decades since, and
answers seem possible now. Perhaps it had nothing to do with drying up.
Maybe it was about that moment where you write a particular piece that
seems so complete you feel you should just let the whole endeavour rest
there. Sometimes you honestly don't have the drive that you had in your
younger years to take up more space.

Of course, it wasn't P.K. Page's last poem. She went on writing and
publishing and receiving awards for a further two decades. For me, though
I never knew her personally, she remains a model—a woman who simply
goes on creating poetry into her oldest years, yet occasionally pauses to
open her hand and say, "This may be enough."

Blaine Marchand

Boy with Umbrella

"Not only have people been forced to flee ... they are now facing new challenges in the camps for displaced people."

MSF 2008 website posting

The stutter of gunfire and vibrato of overhead drones
as his family gathered up their few clothes and sandals
to track along eroded trails and gutted roads
of their valleys, past shattered towns
littered with rounds of spent cartridges,
charred hulks of cars, ruined homes and shops.

He stands on a worn path. On one side the tents
are like foam washed up on the sands of this plateau,
are tethered by a cross-stitch of jute.
On the other, despite the invasion of heat and flies
in a makeshift hospital, doctors
knot sutures that zigzag, truss trauma wounds.

An umbrella, striped in rainbow colours, shadows
blisters on his face and wiry russet hair,
but cannot eclipse his impish grin.
I raise my camera to shoot. He runs away.
The umbrella leaps into the air, descends,
spins, a top orbiting on its axis across the dust.

Splitting Apart

"Breaking stones that block its path,
Splitting the mountain's heart apart."

Sir Mohammed Iqbal, "Saqi Nama"

Dry season. The Indus trickles
past granite rocks blown
to bits in the building
of this highway. Here and
there unearthed chunks
reveal chiselled stickmen,
a flux of animals bearing
antler cornets. A place
of migration? Of herding?
Of hunting down?
Majestic, the rugged peaks
pierce the clouds, sheer
down in deep riven ravines,
sparse embroidery of conifer.
Centuries of monsoon onslaught,
dislodged boulders upended
along cursive shore.
Bright red script, splashed blood.
Graffiti? Diatribe?
Extremist threat?
In my room, light from the lamp flows
down the etched snow-capped massif,
past angular beasts at water's edge,
all glazed around its base. It swells over
my shoulder, pools on the agate
page, the ashen text,
a voice carved out
of this wildness—
This hill stream, my fair Saqi
has a message to give us concerning life.

Blaine Marchand on P.K. Page

The first time I met P.K. Page was in the late 1970s. I was hosting a poetry radio program, called *Sparks 2*, which had replaced a short-lived Ottawa poetry newsletter. I was eager to meet her as I loved her use of imagery, which was so visual, so painterly in my view, and through which she addressed social issues of her youth.

I was also curious as she had lived in Ottawa when, she informed me, she was working for the National Film Board and it was in the city she had met her diplomat husband, W. Arthur Irwin. I was also intrigued by her connection to the gay poet Patrick Anderson and his magazine, *Preview*.

Thirty years later, in 2008, I was posted to the Canadian High Commission in Islamabad, Pakistan. I joined a poetry reading group of Pakistani and British women. I was the only man in the group. I made it my mission to bring the work of Canadian women poets to the group so they could learn more about our literature. Each month I would read a selection by a different poet. Of all the poems I brought, they loved P.K.'s poems the most and asked me to make copies of them so they could read them again at their leisure.

A few months later, by chance, I happened to see P.K. Page's e-mail address on an exchange among a group of poets who were organizing an event in her honour. As she had also lived abroad, I felt an additional connection to her. Although a bit nervous about doing so, I decided to contact her to inform her about the reaction to her poems by the women. To my surprise, she responded saying how much she appreciated my reaching out to her. She confided that in recent years she experienced increased difficulty with writing poetry as her mind no longer seemed to work through imagery. At this point in her life, she added, to know her work still moved people, was most gratifying.

Winged Footprint

1977, Trent University, Peterborough, ON. Pen and ink and colour.

P.K.'s intricate hatchings and cross hatchings in *Winged Footprint*, a mono-chromatic piece, establish exceptional depth and movement. The curvilinear shape and extended lines of her central "footprint," moreover, contribute to the dynamism of the wing motif, a common image in her oeuvre.

Susan McCaslin

A Meditation on P.K. Irwin's pen and ink drawing "Winged Footprint"

> *In all essential particulars writing and painting are interchangeable.*
> *They are alternate roads to silence.*
>
> P.K. Page, "Traveller, Conjurer, Journeyman"

Goddess weather is upon us
a footprint imprints deep space.

Rods and cones dance behind the eyes
but who is the seer, who the seen?

We are up to our galaxies
in affirmation versus denial.

White wings rise from amoeba dark
flapping, gliding, oaring across time

ferrying a cozy nest of ovoid eggs
homeward to resident silence.

Tender stones rock in a dark cabinet
dreaming a fluid geometry.

A flying footprint presses down into planet earth
where heaven and earth embrace

where isness blooms
all in all   a resonant hush.

Susan McCaslin on P.K. Page

Still Waters: P.K. Page's Reservoirs of Silence

In the Fall of 1972, I arrived at the University of Victoria with my fresh MA to assume my first full-time teaching position as a sessional lecturer in the Department of English. I had been writing poetry since childhood and had published in student and literary magazines at university but wasn't active in the poetry scene. Previously, I had attended a reading by P.K. in Vancouver and admired both her person and her poetry but had no idea she was also a visual artist.

When I first attended a P.K. poetry reading, I thought her the most elegant woman I'd ever seen. She stood confidently, hands on hips, exuding an air of mystery. She had the bearing of my maternal grandmother and the eloquence of a wood thrush. Her poetry inspired me to hone my craft. I later found myself looking for a peacock blue silk scarf and dangling hoop earrings like hers.

P.K.'s work encouraged me to experiment with forms such as the glosa, pantoum, and villanelle, though I noted she never abandoned free verse. Each poem attuned listeners not only to the images and metaphors but to the fall and rise of the voice. Yet most of all her work seemed grounded in some unspeakable, unifying, musical silence. I noticed how she played with the analogies between music, the visual arts, images and words. For me her work modelled a balance and synthesis of "higher reason" (or what Dante called "the good of intellect") and imagination.

As I developed my own engagement with various mystical traditions, including Sufism, I was delighted to discover more about P.K.'s Islamic explorations and practices. When I landed a full-time position in the English Department at Douglas College, I showed my students a National Film Board of Canada documentary film titled *Still Waters: The Poetry of P.K. Page* (1990), where she reflects on the place behind the eyes where all things flow from stillness.

In 1995, I was ecstatic when Richard Olafson of Ekstasis Editions published my first trade book (*Locutions*). Up till then my husband and I had self-published some of my early chapbooks. In 1997, I entered a sequence of poems titled *Letters to William Blake* in [M]other Tongue Publishing's Annual Chapbook Competition. To my surprise, the sequence was awarded first place and published as a chapbook set on a handset press by Mona Fertig and Peter Haase. The award meant all the more because the judging was "blind" and the judge P.K. Page. Looking back, it's clear that P.K.'s endorsement of my work at that crucial stage in my life encouraged me to remain on the poetry path and continue to open to the wellsprings of the creative imagination.

Throughout the decades since those early days, I attended readings by P.K. when she came to Vancouver. At one of the last of these in 2004 at the Vancouver Public Library toward the end of P.K.'s life, I approached her after the reading to ask her to sign my book. Since we hadn't been in touch for a number of years, I opened by saying, "You may not remember me but…" Out of her remarkable generosity, P.K. took both my hands, looked directly into my eyes, and said, "Of course I remember you, Susan."

Now at the age of seventy-five, I find myself delving into her work again, this time spending more time with her drawings, geometrical designs, sketches, and paintings, still astonished that such a rare integration of the art forms is possible. I ask, where do the poems, the paintings, and the music come from? How did she constantly tap the "still waters" of a resonant silence?

Viewing the film *Still Waters* once again, I am struck by how P.K. speaks at its end about climate change and the impending doom we face due to human exploitation of planet earth. She ends with these prescient words: "From everything I've read, if we don't change our ways our planet is doomed…. I'm really wondering how to serve my planet at this point. And I feel all of us should be addressing this. It seems the most serious thing I've ever had to confront in my life."[1]

---

1 *Still Waters: The Poetry of P.K. Page*. Directed by Donald Winkler. 1990; Ottawa, Ontario: National Film Board of Canada. nfb.ca/film/still_waters/.

Susan McMaster

Dorveille

Entre les mers,
dormir, reveiller,
between two seas
of sleep and rise,
a waking haze
pale and dark,
wrapped, entwined,
partnered in steps
where poetry hums
in lolling waves
of words and song.
Here Dante began
his purgatory tale,
here Emily wrote
to a stumbling buzz,
here Virginia filled
and loosed her pen,
here language
melds, bodies melt,
warmth glows to swell,
limbs stir, subside,
hearts call and recall
without words or sight,
answer with breath,
with closed seeking eyes,
then turn, return
to re-enter rest—
la mort, la vie,
a dowsing dream,
la mer entière
of passing death.

Susan McMaster

These Are the Poems of Age

These are the poems
of age, the plain
spoken ones that have no
ecstasies to offer,
no wild
metaphors to twist
frontal lobes,
massage cerebellums,
astound hormones
into fight or flight.

Just words. A few,
to say—

sometimes gratitude
overwhelms melancholy—

sometimes despair
is joy upside
down, and a word
can flip it—

sometimes I wait for you
here in my soft bed
and know
you will come.

Susan McMaster on P.K. Page

How does influence, the flux and flow of idea and thought, feeling and care, creep in, insinuate, soak, slip, slide, ingratiate, simply enter the course of a life from another life, even from far away? Living in Ottawa, I only met P.K. Page once or twice. I read her poems, but we never talked about them, or about mine. So, is she a mentor?

To a poet, I think, the words themselves can be more of a mentor than any words about words. I thought of this when I offered "Dorveille" for this anthology, because its subject is the half dreaming space between first and second sleep that often nourishes writers. P.K. wove lyrical spells with her "bright glimpse[s] of beauty striking like a bell / so that the whole may toll," and the musical elements of "Dorveille" echo her invitation into the shimmering, elusive and delusive, immersive world of poetry.

At the same time, P.K.'s words were always concise, even dry and sharp, and this only grew more evident as she aged—"the dead or the near dead / are now all knucklebone"—plain language that speaks to me in "These are the poems of age," written as I enter my seventh decade.

P.K., I didn't know you, but your graceful, powerful phrases live for me in a corner somewhere lit with joy and calm and wise understanding, and I often sit in that sunlight as I write.

kjmunro

Three Haiku

directed to & inspired by P.K. Page's "Star-Gazer"

constellations
painted on the ceiling
no words

*

my finger
along the line of page
a satellite

*

dark night
every raindrop a star
falling

kjmunro on P.K. Page

A memory—at the launch of the anthology *Why I Sing the Blues*, edited by Jan Zwicky & Brad Cran, at the Vancouver Writers Fest (in 2001), I believe it was Jay Ruzesky who read P.K.'s poem. It is called "Empty House Blues" & the line about the house crying out at night catches me every time.

Angels

1957, PRIVATE COLLECTION, TORONTO, ON. GOUACHE AND EGG TEMPERA.

The poet A. J. M. Smith once encouraged P.K. to illustrate her poems; *Angels* is one of the few examples of her heeding his advice, as it illustrates the poem "Images of Angels," published in her earlier collection *The Metal and the Flower* (1954). The painting portrays the poem's angel figures, "part daisy in a white manshape," as they gather "on the Elysian grass / playing ring-around-a-rosy" (*Kaleidoscope*, 73).

Susan Musgrave

After Enlightenment

My old love tries to open the door
carrying two buckets of red paint.
The lesson for today—let it go.
Not until you have first put down
whatever you desire most. But you
don't do you—you try to grasp
the doorknob when your hands
are already full of split
cedar for the stove, or water
hauled from the well in a leaky pot
(by the time you reach the house
there's scarcely a drop left). Hard
to let go of such habits that cause us
to bow under their weight, let go

of a life. Put it down. Red paint rivering
the sky and the blistering stars. No water
within reach to put the flames out.

Not Enough

The smooth stone does not say
to the jagged ocean, you are
not enough; the kingfisher
to the shining, twisting fish
in his beak, you are not enough.
The knife does not say
to the cutting board, you are
not enough. Where does this
message come from, the one
the mind says to the rest
of the body, daily, as we struggle to live
on this earth: you are never enough.

Tenderness

Two kingfishers fly into plate glass
windows at opposite ends of my house
in the same moment: what
are the odds? I expect they had been flying
towards one another for thousands of miles,
across centuries, or at least from opposite
sides of the river. No matter: same outcome.
Two bodies committed to the ground,
the hard ground, no time for prayer.
Does anyone care that I sit here paralyzed
with tenderness? Don't think
for a moment anybody cares. Suffering
only comes in two kinds. Yours.
And mine.

Susan Musgrave on P.K. Page

In lieu of an anecdote, a dream. Stephen Reid (my husband) has died and his body will be in an open coffin in a church and we are all waiting to see him but the coffin never quite arrives (lots of obstacles, like trying to park a car that I am in with P.K. Page.) I say to P.K. "I'm going to write a book that will teach people how to steal cars. You shouldn't steal a new car, that's too obvious. You should always steal some kind of an old beater."

P.K. says, "That's one book I'm glad I won't have to read."

Lynne Mustard on Reading P.K. Page

I often feel that P.K. Page perfected the art and science (fiction) of teleportation. For example, her phrase, "The feel of walking smooth in my summer legs," instantly transports me to those long-ago, carefree days of being a teenager, striding around my world in short shorts.

And then there's, "They contract tenderness from each other like disease and talk as if each word had just been born—a butterfly, and soft from its cocoon." That sentence stops me, stills me, suspends me. Then it whisks me to that magical realm of awe and wonder which talent, of all kinds, can conjure. It doesn't seem to matter to me whether the adept is a writer, an opera singer, an artist or a prescient goalie diving blindly to where the puck will be. I am moved by, and thankful for, the talent and skill on display.

Lynne Mustard

Recognition

The Art of P.K. Irwin: observer, other, Gemini
falls open to page eight

and there I am on the vellum—
in a somewhat sympathetic piece

p.k., being kind, called it, "Untitled. 1959"
but it's really a portrait of me

a creature of awkward angles
wearing, as fascinator, a puffball of blown-out seeds

and there's my updo, bristling with sardines
along with my dragon eye, my unicorn horn, my grin

this sketch of my innermost alien self
could not feel more accurate

patsy, pat, patricia, p.k., the startling, intuitive artist
channeled my unseen

Untitled 1959

PRIVATE COLLECTION. INK.

This is one of a series of ink drawings which P.K. created towards the end of her time in Brazil. Like the others in the series it is quite unlike the more familiar colourful representational works of the period and foreshadows the biomorphic abstractions of the Mexican period.

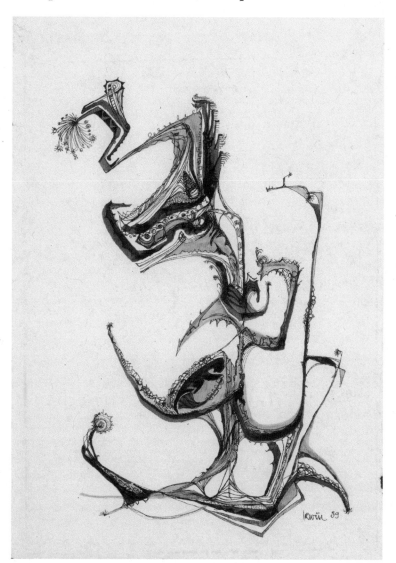

Ulrike Narwani

Choir Me Too

an extended glosa

And choir me too to keep my heart a size
larger than seeing, unseduced by each
bright glimpse of beauty striking like a bell,
so that the whole may toll,
its meaning shine
clear of the myriad images that still—
do what I will—encumber its pure line.

> P.K. Page, "After Rain"

On foggy days, when the heart's
seeing is cramped and narrow,
may the baton of early morning,
stroke by stroke, woo
my sluggish form, call forth
a crescendo of light until sky's
soprano ringing white
springs open my wings
into flight. May sun's rise
choir me too to keep my heart a size

larger than seeing, unseduced by
the passing day's gift of silver air
that pleasures earth's rusty leaves
until they shine, by rainbow's sigh
arcing indigo, blue, green, yellow,
orange, red, the many-timbred swell
a faint promise of lift against dark sky.
Unseduced by lilac spring, the blossom
splurge, the fragrant petal's short-lived spell—
each *bright glimpse of beauty striking like a bell*

so that the whole may toll.
Was it in Sidney-by-the-Sea
that you, P.K., said this so well?
I sat at the back in Galleon's Books
and Antiques next to gold-rimmed china.
Heard a voice, soft, benign,
winding past shawled shoulders,
words of porcelain-thin beauty
that conjure a deeper chime.
May *its meaning shine*

clear of the myriad images that still—
even as fog thickens
and the foghorn sounds lost,
fill the loose sleeve of my life:
a tree's branches bouncing with baby raccoons,
an eagle taking wing from a resinous pine,
rhododendrons crimson with pendulous blooms,
images that still ... do what I will,
vibrate like a tuning fork's tine,
encumber my heart's *pure line.*

Ulrike Narwani on P.K. Page

It must have been around the year 2003. I had recently moved to Sidney, BC, on Vancouver Island after having lived abroad for many years. I was eager to take advantage of any interesting cultural opportunities that presented themselves. At that time, readings by well-known writers were taking place in different locations in the town, in Tanner's Bookstore, for instance. On this particular night, someone called P.K. Page was due to give a poetry reading in Galleon's Books and Antiques.

Although I had studied literature many years ago, I knew very little about Canadian literature, and nothing of its poetry. I had no idea who P.K. Page was. It was a miserable, cold and rainy night. I was late, so when I entered the store, I could only find a seat close to the entrance. Chairs were dispersed among tables filled with displays of fine china, books, and assortments of nautical antiques. The place was packed. Where was P.K.? It was only when I heard voices somewhere at the very back of the store, that I was able to zero in. Peering past all the heads, and hats, and shawls, I saw a grey-haired lady seated in a low chair. She spoke quietly. I could barely hear her. But something stayed with me. I remembered her, this moment, this night.

I learned more about her later at the Planet Earth Poetry Reading Series in Victoria, the name, of course, derived from P.K.'s poem "Planet Earth." I learned that one of her favourite forms in poetry was the glosa—one voice conversing with another. And, that her voice, embedded as it was in a particular place and time, called on us to keep our hearts "larger than seeing." Perhaps it was this call I heard that evening, inspiring, so many years later, my response.

Leonard Neufeldt

Covent Garden

Your attention is outward,
thrust like an immigrant into the public sweat
of anonymity, disorder of bodies,
and raw gargle of sounds
you want to agree with despite jet-lag
catatonia, threat of evening rain
and a cue across the street. Pirouette
of Bahama-white boat shoes, calf-length
trousers black as the high-hitch
of suspenders, and twists by two
chalk faces stutter-juggling even as
longing gives notice next to you:
long-limbed singers, metronomed
arias and duets from *Cosi Fan Tutte*,
the orchestra a finger-fidgeting
electronic keyboard almost aced
by a pigeon spooked away
by the gritty havoc of a cell-phone
argument behind you.
Into the upturned hat a Drury Lane drunk's
largesse, pennies nameless
as your bank withdrawal in the pocket
of the coat your daughter donated last week
to her charity auction, a matter
still to be worked out

The opera house and yawning
Transport Museum may want to offer
other streets and directions from tomorrow
or the London of last time
in order to find you
with a Mozart of pure play,
mordents and trills spot-on,
less face-up juggling, body not going
wrong as yours, short breath felt
in passersby fashionably dressed
or plain as breakfast porridge and kippers
and lacking any desire to hide
their perfect grace as they look your way

Leonard Neufeldt on P.K. Page

We all know literary artists who have written the same kind of work repeatedly. Not P.K., whose works were always on the move as she herself was, in her interests and physical as well as cultural sojourning. I can't name a quintessential P.K. volume or composition. There is so much to value about her life and works, but their openendedness is what I particularly admire.

Bright Fish

1960, TRENT UNIVERSITY, PETERBOROUGH, ON. ETCHING AND AQUATINT. PRINT 5/12.

P.K. spent much of her time in New York City learning the art of printmaking, first at the Pratt Institute in 1959, and then at the Art Students League under the direction of the infamous Harry Sternberg when she returned in the fall of 1960. According to her *Mexican Journal,* she much preferred working with Sternberg, whom she found to be "clear and logical" (83). Her interest in printmaking, however, waned as she found the medium to be "too complicated" (87). Nevertheless, she managed to create a couple of fine plates and numerous prints from this period, including this *Bright Fish* etching and aquatint print.

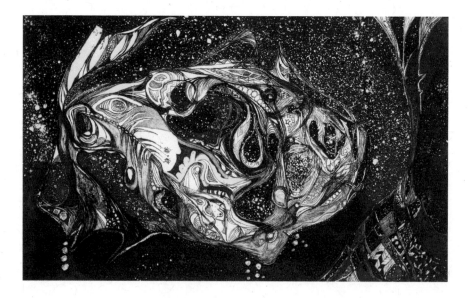

Barbara Colebrook Peace

Dziekanski as a Map of Canada

(In memoriam Robert Dziekanski: April 15, 1967–October 14, 2007)

But we were wrong and the map was true
    P.K. Page, "The Map"

We remember you in autumn, when spawning salmon leap
in rivers, their brightness seeking home.
Everywhere the arc of your falling body:
we know it in the waterfalls,
the hump of the mountains and the landslide to the wet, slick road.
You lie now like one of the maps
you spread out before your journey here:

your fingers clasp the eastern boundary at Cape Spear;
your hair billows among jellyfish;
humpback whales rise and fall with your slumping back.
Just before your last breath, the moon
moves closer to earth and leans against us.
If we follow the moon's path
across the land, lake after lake, forest after forest, we see

how you most fit the Rocky Mountains,
how your shoulders scar upward, how they
lift your questions to the sky. An avalanche groans
and your eyes open wide, on guard under stars
that belong to no one.
We listen to your anguish rockfall through canyons.
But when we follow the stone trail

westward to the western boundary, we touch
your feet. Now they are part of the rocks
at the base of Mount Saint Elias, outcroppings
among the stones that gather round our stories;
like the day we recognised Kwäday Dän Ts'ìnchi,
Long Ago Person Found, his name
a strange stumble, like yours, on our tongues.

Barbara Colebrook Peace on P.K. Page

P.K. Page was and is an "extraordinary presence," a phrase she used in her poem "Presences." An extraordinary presence when she was here on earth, and now that she's no longer physically here, still an extraordinary presence. For me personally, a presence not only in her writings and art but sometimes in my night-time dreams of flight. This is interesting because P.K. herself talked to me about her flying dreams. Dreaming, there's an intense feeling of connection with the Earth and its beauty. Sometimes, P.K. speaks a few words of mystery, encouragement or wisdom, and I wake profoundly moved.

My poem in this anthology shares P.K.'s interest in maps and their meanings, an interest which appears in several of her poems, prose writings and works of art. I wrote about this interest in a book review: "Page's thinking about herself and her identity was not the usual sort; she was asking the question on a different level than simply trying to situate herself as a woman or Canadian or ambassador's wife or poet, writer, artist. She was asking how 'I' bring something into being; asking who is the self who engages in perception; asking about the multiple selves; asking about the relation of the temporal self to eternity; asking about the individual spirit in relation to the unmapped infinite. { …..} But because her life was externally so successful, the surprise for the reader may be to discover how much Page had to overcome, of loneliness and discouragement, and of finding a way where there were no maps." *

Elsewhere, I've written about something which has meant a great deal to me in my life and in my writing, P.K. Page's ability to evoke the invisible dimensions of eternity in terms of this beloved planet: "Praise, shadow, and dimensions of eternity are so interwoven in her work that we return from reading her poetry with the sense of a much larger world than the one we normally inhabit. A shadow world within a golden world; a golden world within a shadow world. Page gives us hope for this planet and hope for the self, world within world, in which we live against the stellar background of the cosmos. The words she once wrote of the embodied self, 'It has a leafy smell / of being young in all the halls of heaven,' might aptly be spoken of her poetry, for it is both of the earth and of eternity." **

*excerpted from a review by Barbara Colebrook Peace in *BC Studies*, November 2013, of *Journey with No Maps: A Life of P.K. Page* by Sandra Djwa.

**excerpted from an essay by Barbara Colebrook Peace and Kelly Parsons, in *P.K. Page: Essays on Her Works* edited by Linda Rogers and Barbara Colebrook Peace (Guernica, 2001).

Barbara Pelman

Homage to P.K. Page

And newly in love,
we must draw it and paint it
our pencils and brushes and loving caresses
smoothing the holy surfaces.

        P.K. Page, "Planet Earth"

That day you called the school
I was teaching the glosa to my Grade 12 students.
That week we had painted lines from your poem
on the downtown hoardings:
O this great beloved world and all the creatures in it.
You called to thank us, you who had taught us
to put word beside word, to reach down the stanza
until we found yours and other poets' words,
nine lines then the other, the beautiful borrowed lines.
And newly in love

We wrote glosas, and demi-glosas, only half the work
or so we thought, and we opened poetry books
to find four lines that said, yes, use me,
I will help you make a poem, and they did,
though my glosas never rhymed, and you chided me.
Keep to the form, you said, rhyme the sixth line
with the ninth, make it sing to the tenth line,
the borrowed one, and some of us
took pencils and brushes, knowing
we must draw it and paint it

for is this not our first muse, our Mother, each leaf
gold or crimson, drenched with autumn rain,
robins and juncos on the hunt, bright moon
between the branches, and on the shore
the tides pull and stretch, driftwood edged in kelp
and the sky—didn't you tell us? *such an O overhead*
how we must burnish and polish and shine it,
attend to its blessings, each marvelous detail,
our pencils and brushes and loving caresses

relearning the iridescent flower beetle, the blue dragon
nudibranch, mandarinfish, golden pheasant,
long tailed widowbird, the panther, the bonobo,
and the trees—arbutus, its golden limbs, weeping willow,
even the names a blessing on the tongue.
We search for the words, your glosas to guide us,
attentive to detail, fingers on the keyboard, coaxing and praising,
celebrating the feathers, the fur, the meadows, the mountains,
the wine-dark sea, each shining pebble,
smoothing the holy surfaces.

Barbara Pelman

Cello

> *When he asked if I still loved him, I didn't answer;*
> *but of course, I loved him.*
> *He'd become, by then, like the rhyme scheme between lost*
> *and most.*
>
> Carl Phillips, "In a Field at Sunset"

There was a boy, in Germany, one summer,
he spoke halting English, and I had no German
but we were young enough not to care.
It was August, and along the Spree River,
there was a cello playing. He asked me to dance
and of course, because it was summer, in Germany,
and we were young, I did, and after many days
and nights, we were still humming the tunes from that cello.
I saw him again, just yesterday, so many years later.
When he asked if I still loved him, I didn't answer.

Could I fold the years back? Seal them against time,
which disturbs all the moments we thought we had.
Did we kiss? Of course. Did we talk?
There were times when the silence between us
was richer than words, heavier and deeper, as if I knew him
from some other life, but as I said, we were young
and I am less wise now with all my years. Perhaps
the trees leaning into the river, the tall grasses
remember better, those hours after the cello.
But of course, I loved him.

He read me Rilke, I read him Yeats.
Because we had no language, we listened more carefully,
the words rising and falling, like music.
Was it hours or years ago? The sun on our backs,
the sharp grasses, dragonflies drifting above us,
the languid scent of our bodies, deliquescent sun,
such words that could stretch along his skin,
his lustrous skin, his eyes solemn, so liquid
he could fill me up. But as I said, I am less wise now,
He'd become, by then, like the rhyme scheme between lost—

and ghost, and I try with words
to pull that summer sun onto the page,
the long days by the river,
his hands, his spine, the curve of his neck,
the way he woke my skin. And later, at night,
was that an owl, that low gurgle in the trees above us?
And beyond that, the inescapable something
that halts my steps now, along a dark city street
elsewhere and so many years later, someone I loved the briefest
and most.

Barbara Pelman on P.K. Page

I never really met P.K. Page, not in person. Only her voice over a phone and a couple of letters. I had brought my students downtown to write lines of poems on the hoardings around one of the construction sites. A day of paint and excitement, favourite passages memorized, books of poetry held open, now with red and green thumbprints. One student wrote: "O this great beloved earth and all the creatures in it," from P.K.'s gorgeous glosa, "Planet Earth." It made the Monday morning paper. Well into the second class of the morning, I received a phone call. Usually, the secretaries field all calls so that teachers don't get interrupted, but one wise secretary, upon hearing it was P.K. Page, patched it through immediately.

"Thank you for using my poem," she said, and we talked for a good ten minutes while I directed my students to keep writing in their journals.

"I teach glosas all the time," I said, "and use your work, particularly that one, and "Love's Pavilion." I make all my students write glosas." Then I modestly told her that I love to write glosas, love the paradoxical freedom you find within a framework, a form.

"Send me some of your glosas," she offered, and gave me her address.

"Well," I said to my students after hanging up the phone, "that was the author of the poems we have just read. Well done, Marcella! (she was the student who chose those lines) You see how poetry is alive," I told them. "How it connects."

I did send her my poems, and she gently chastised me for not using the rhyme scheme in lines 6 and 9. She then sent me a few of the poems that were going into her new book of glosas, *Coals and Roses*. Precious gifts. Generous gifts.

That was in the fall. She died in January and I never got to meet her or beg for her autograph, or to share more glosas. But I told that story to all my students for the next few years I taught at Reynolds before I retired. How a poet will reach out to you when you honour their work, how the sharing of poetry—the writing of it, the love of it—is part of the connective tissue that holds us all together. And these days, glosas are my favourite things to write. They usually happen when I find a poem I love, or some lines that reach deeply, then I work on constructing a poem around those lines. It's fascinating and challenging to see how the borrowed words can be folded into your own, as seamlessly as possible, as if you had written them yourself. An honouring.

Though, apologies P.K., I seldom bother to rhyme them.

Evening Dance

c. 1993, private collection, Saanichton, BC. Scratched oil pastel.

Evening Dance illustrates P.K.'s poem "Evening Dance of the Grey Flies," first published in her collection of the same title in 1981. The poem opens with the image of "Grey flies, fragile slender-winged and slender-legged" who "scribble a pencilled script across the sunlit lawn." In *Evening Dance*, P.K. has scratched the flies' "script" into a teal sky as the sunlight "gilds their frail / bodies, makes them fat and bright as bees" (*Kaleidoscope*, 151).

Pamela Porter

Solstice

> *each bright glimpse of beauty striking like a bell,*
> *so that the whole world may toll.*
>> P.K. Page, "After Rain"

This winter is all silvered moon and stars, small birds printing
runes into snow, hieroglyph of horses' hooves
frozen in the mud, rimmed in crystalled petals of ice.
Ancient, this world, these fields gone white—a cumulous sky,
each bright glimpse of beauty striking like a bell,

so we may teach ourselves to be whole, and holy
as moonlit lamps of Queen Anne's lace,
so that a whiteness deeper than any of us can know
may shroud the earth to be reborn, and in us a green belled wonder,
so that the whole world may toll.

Pamela Porter on P.K. Page

I never met P.K. in person but heard through writer Beryl Young that Beryl had given P.K. a copy of my novel in verse, *The Crazy Man,* and the two of them had a nice discussion over it. Apparently P.K. quite liked the book.

The reason I used her two lines in my poem was that I was looking through some of P.K.'s work and the lines resonated with me. I might not have written the poem at all except that we'd had a fairly significant snowfall one winter Saturday and the power went out, and my son Drew and I were the only ones home that weekend, and as it turned out, that day was voting day for municipal elections, and Drew, who had just turned eighteen, shoveled the driveway as well as a clear path to the end of our cul-de-sac, just so we could go vote. It took him three hours. That was enough time for me to write the poem. It must have been around the winter solstice, hence, the title. He's a lawyer now and remains a fervent voter.

DC Reid

Love at Yellow Point Lodge

> *They are why we sleep*
> *and why upon waking, bewildered by the day,*
> *the white lions rise with us in the sun*
> *and move with great patience toward the mind*
>
> Patrick Lane, "White Lions in the Afternoon"

They are why we sleep
these August days, drowning, swift and deep.
Truth is all provisional, happiness
is in the viscera, something to keep,
the gift of screws and more worthy than gold.
The beautiful endures,
this tawny fur, rangy in my hand.
How to scratch the ear of a lion
unflinching at its rumbled pleasure?
I eat peaches insatiably

and why upon waking, bewildered by the day
do I remember a hand ripped off in a casual way?
A hand may hold an arm, feel out
the bifurcate furrows of sandstone that lay
sweltering in the sun's love. Here you come
slendering the sandstone in lemon stockings
that go all the way to here,
lady who never photographs twice the same,
whose body is a magnet, whose mind is irresistible.
Here I am, hands in pockets in love, and now

the white lions rise with us in the sun,
chessmen advancing the sandstone run.
I no longer desire protection thick enough for pain.
The world we left strips like skin.
We know the bed we will share this first time
away from families, in a breathless world.

Decisions have a bitterness we taste
to be who we are: the rasp of a feline tongue
rips off skin and brings forth sweetness.
Hold me like a peach

and move with great patience toward the mind.
Walking our mountain of years, we might find
the sea in all its sluicing goes where it goes,
you with slippers in your hand.
What I know is this:
when burned I spread on ointment
and walk around the fire.
White lions walk with me, waist high, Victorian,
a tree the shape of lightning, and you
lady in lemon stockings that go all the way to here.

Nothing Better than Blinding the Beautiful

Whoever has no house now will never have one.
Whoever is alone will stay alone
will sit, read, write long letters through the evening
and wander on the boulevards, up and down…

    Rainer Maria Rilke, "Autumn Day"

whichever side it is on. A black thing
with its implacable face.
To avoid it you
will tell yourself you are something,

    P.K. Page, "Autumn"

Whoever has no house now will never have one.
Nothing better than blinding the beautiful one.
I'll jag Persinger's spot, right hemisphere, just
there. An electric finger makes you come
until you know *Him,* makes you rapture some
languages you cannot speak, yet you speak them.'
The vision of dreams when you know
the cinemascope of your skull is a leafing
jungle or a curtain, or a hanging cloth
made to define the staging
whichever side it is on, a black thing.

Whoever is alone will stay alone.
Your generic face rises like a moon,
or sleeping drone real as any dream
or thought not entered. Say a moan
so golden you are mistaken for her brother.
Forget the sun that is a sharpness in your eyes.
And that crack where the light shines in
makes a waterfall of blood. Trace
the sludge of blood and broken platelets.
A little canon will blast it off. And grace,
with its implacable face

will sit, read, write long letters through the evening.
An equation of loneliness or longing
which is the wrong place to start for
happiness, say, of a white flying thing
you see un-cynically, lands in the camellia
with its pink wax flowers it sheds
almost as they breathe in early spring.
And grass is stubble on a face, a brief
and surly face, but just a face without
a thought, or image to conceive.
To avoid it you leave

And wander on the boulevards, up and down.
Close your eyes so you cannot see you frown.
Close the doors so you cannot escape you down
the pages of books in dander piles in brown
rooms of veiny light strained
through leaves of stereoscopic green.
Try the nitrogen of your company,
the hydrogen of your bathing.
And a mirror, a pot top,
a silver fingernail, and a ring
will tell yourself you are something.

Joan Marie Roberts

A Life As We Know It

All italicized words in this ghazal are the titles of P.K. Page poems.

Whether *The Mole,* the owl, or the shimmer of fish,
all have beginning, a connection, a wish.

The Answer half hidden; no story untold.
A blessing, a challenge, a friend of pure gold.

As Ten, As Twenty, as fifty love-days
to write a fine script, an intuitive play.

A Unit of Five, maybe nine give a nod.
The trail of the Sufi, the traveler abroad.

An honour received, a *Children's Hymn* heard.
An energy of love, amazement and word.

Joan Marie Roberts on P.K. Page

The charm of the landscape of P.K.'s childhood in the Alberta foothills and prairie and later in the rugged Winnipeg climate brought to light her formative years with nature.

This we have in common—I know these regions well.

And to top it off we were both babies living in Red Deer, Alberta, while our fathers served in the military. What are the odds?!!

So, of course, I delight in the possibility that the drinking water held a special potion that inspired the poet to surface in P.K. and hopefully in me as well.

Jay Ruzesky

Afterlife, She Said

for P.K. Page

She wanted to look at death, dark chicken of
doom with razor claws; she wanted
to approach with her eyes open. She
said she was not afraid of
death. Said she was not
afraid of lions either, although she
might change her mind if there was
one in the room.

And in the moment, well, perhaps she
stepped onto the tail of a comet like it
was an escalator of glory. Or, as was the
way with some sages, rode away to
heaven on an ox or boar or whale. We
didn't see it happen.

After, she said, she would, if there
was a way, send signs. I was talking
about M. whom I had not seen for
years, and that day I ran into her
in the shopping mall. My wife
dreamed of peaches and found
a pie delivered by a friend the
next morning. My hands grew
aware of each other. A hummingbird
whispered in my ear. Coincidences
all, and they faded after a few weeks.

I wonder now about the dimensions she
imagined. We can not *not* see
what has been revealed to us.

And thinking about
her these years later as I
hang laundry on the
line, the brights *are*
brighter; the
whites
whiter

Jay Ruzesky on P.K. Page

P.K. Page should be remembered for her facility with language. There are plenty of good poets around these days, but P.K.'s writing has greatness. She's someone we should be reading two and five hundred years from now (if there is a *then* and a *we* that far down the road). In her lifetime she saw Canadian poetry blossom from the handful of practitioners who were writing in Canada when she was young, to the rich, truly multicultural net of Canadian poets we can point to now and she was happy to see it. She also saw the looming threats to the planet that have only increased since she left us. Although she was older than me by half a century she treated me as if we were peers in poetry and her friendship is one of the things in my life I hold most dear.

One of my favourite things about spending time with P.K. was the way she would stop in the middle of a sentence to consider a word or phrase. She could be describing something as "immaculate" and then she would stop abruptly, look up and say, "If something can be 'immaculate,' then is there such a thing as 'maculate'?"

And, of course, there is.

Excalibur's Handle

1971-2, PRIVATE COLLECTION, VICTORIA, BC. PUNCH AND GOUACHE.

P.K. created *Excalibur's Handle* while in Hawaii, where she and her husband, Arthur Irwin, took an extended vacation following a heart attack he had suffered in November of 1971. It was here that P.K. began to experiment with punches, a technique she no doubt learned from Pat Martin Bates, P.K.'s close friend and artist renowned for perforating her works with a hat pin. In an article she wrote on Bates's work, published just prior to her trip to Hawaii, P.K. reflected on this technique, calling it a kind of "tattooing… an initiation rite to mark a turning point," noting that such "rituals of transformation are usually accompanied by ordeals" ("Darkinbad" 39). Page's own punches, and *Excalibur's Handle*, the title referencing the hilt of the magical sword that transformed the mythical Arthur into a King, symbolize a spiritual transmutation following her and Arthur's personal ordeal.

Lesley Strutt

Weeding

> *The wax has melted*
> *but the dream of flight*
> *persists.*

> P.K. Page, "This Heavy Craft"

Lao Tzu visits me in the garden,
finds me on my knees, brow furrowed.
He compliments me on my weeding,
laughs tenderly.

At first I don't get the joke.
Then I laugh too, sit back on my heels,
toss my spade into the air.
Where it falls I begin again.

Lesley Strutt on P.K. Page

I first read poetry by P.K. Page in my high school Canadian poetry anthology, in the 1960's. She was one of two women included in the anthology. I was impressed. She was a woman and a poet. Her poetry, with its spare line and vivid imagery, has continued to guide and challenge me throughout my poetry writing life.

Cynthia Woodman Kerkham

Late Summer in Frederick Arm

> *They call all experience of the senses 'mystic',*
> *when the experience is considered.*
> *So an apple becomes mystic when I taste in it*
> *the summer and the snows, the wild welter of earth*
> *and the insistence of the sun.*
>
> DH Lawrence, "Mystic"

Here at the head of the crucifix, Frederick Arm
flows into Nodales Channel; Cordero is the crosspiece.
A week anchored at a half-drowned dock.
Frederick was a British explorer, but the name
is known to me from a child's tale of a mouse
who spends his hours slow-gathering nuts and noticing
the gauze of dusk's mayfly over the lake's smooth cheek.
His neighbours scurry about their work;
chastise Frederick's laziness; make their disapproval heard.
They call all experience of the senses 'mystic', when the experience is considered.

The Frederick in me wonders this morning how to translate
the preening of herring gulls lined on a log—
chatter of croaks and caws, tweets and quacks
that must be about fish, and the obstinacy of tick under wing.
Into silence comes the click of alder leaves as they tumble gold
amongst evergreen; the skritch of gravel on logging roads;
a rockslide's distant, throaty rumble.
How know we are alive if not in the noticing?
In an abandoned orchard, sit.
So an apple becomes mystic when I taste in it

the drip of glaciers, granite dust
and tart sun. Or in the flesh
of Esturo Basin trout the taste
of water grasses, sweet lake, a dusting of sea.
I soak in this elemental place:

its lightness of spirit and aura of limitless days.
Float in the wild silence where all the Fredericks
can stretch their reach beyond the business of living;
can pull into eyes' and lungs' full girth,
the summer and the snows, the wild welter of earth.

Each hour skims magic
like phosphorescence in a night sea.
Here senses rule. And Fredericks
store their visions for the telling in the long winters,
when the seeds are nearly spent,
when the dark cave closes in,
and trapped mice seek the value
of experience considered; then Frederick will rise,
recount tug of unfurling leaf, green smell of ocean,
and the insistence of the sun.

Cynthia Woodman Kerkham on reading P.K. Page

P.K. Page came to me along with the sound of water. I'd heard her read a few times in the nineties and been struck by her lilting voice, her elegant delivery, her wit, and the power and economy of language in her poems, at once precise and elastic. One summer, while sailing in Desolation Sound, I read a lot of P.K.'s poetry and memorized some poems, including one by D.H. Lawrence called "Mystic." Poetry magic being what it is, when I needed to write about what I was seeing around me, four lines of the Lawrence poem came together along with a fairy tale and P.K. Page. Her sense of structure, and in this case the structure of the glosa, gave shape to what I wanted to say.

Over the years of reading P.K. Page's poems, I've been struck by her invention and use of new modes of poetic expression. I'm indebted to her, as many poets and readers are. This is what we mean by the power of language to touch and inspire: P.K. Page swayed beside me those many summers on the waters of the Pacific, navigating for a fellow wordsmith with her gifts.

Derk Wynand

Sandpipers

What are you looking for? Stupid
question and who besides

is asking whom? A flock
of sandpipers, nervously,

unflocks. Their general drift
remains: sand to water, water

to sand, and you almost begin
to get it. What *they* are seeking

seems sure, food, not food
for thought, ocean water

to your mirage. They glide
along the foaming edge

while your mind, even
as it thinks it wanders, sticks

in the sand. The birds
use their legs to stay

levelheaded, inclined only
toward their want.

Derk Wynand on P.K. Page

I don't have any poem directly *inspired* by P.K., but I did read her "Poor Bird" at Open Space in a memorial for her some years ago, and my own "Sandpipers." Sandra Djwa thought I caught P.K.'s voice well when I read "Poor Bird." Did I catch her *spirit* with "Sandpipers"? Dunno. She had a big spirit and it soared.

The Dance

1963, Trent University, Peterborough, ON. Egg tempera on board.

The Dance was P.K.'s favourite piece in her oeuvre. She was inspired to paint it following a visit to the Fu-Shing Chinese Opera in January 1963, which she called "one of the outstanding events of my life" in her journal. She was particularly struck by the opening of the performance, which featured a red carpet rolled out against a plain black backdrop, and the intricate, multicolored costumes and headdresses, which moved about to the music as if "in another 'space'" or a "molecular" world (*Mexican Journal*, 203). P.K. uses egg tempera to capture the brilliant colours of the Opera, while her *sgraffito* technique emulates the rhythmic movement of the "dance" through its varied, curvilinear forms scratched into the surface of the paint. Charles Seliger's influence is palpable here in P.K.'s intricate and detailed patterning of organic forms suggesting the infinite space of molecular worlds within worlds.

Anna Yin

Purple and Gold

In Memory of P.K. Page

lines in italics are from P.K. Page, "The Metal and The Flower" and
Journey with No Maps: A Life of P.K. Page *by Sandra Djwa*

Your life is a purple pearl
sent from the old Kingdoms
to the long West Coast.
Your childhood rides on horseback
with irises, bluebells and lavender
all purple in purple clouds.

Your married life, a lucky star,
glides from one destination to another.
The exotic winds mix your nostalgia
and talents, open a world of wonders.

But what do I know?
How does
black and white at midnight glow
this garden of barbed wire and roses?
What is the life in a shell?
What kind of waves are calling?

Yet I do know—
your poetry is the gold
beyond time and space.
It speaks of the colour of harvest,
and the weight of life
where you see *two divine moons,*
and the cure for *Planet Earth.*

Extracting from streams of life,
refining through the fire of passions,
you crown us with the power
and beauty of words
where *our third eye* sees:
gold shining from the underground,
roses rising from purple dreams.
Under *the Sky Tree,*
you find the way home.

Anna Yin on P.K. Page

Traveller, What Do You Seek?

In Memory of P.K. Page

I read P.K. Page's poetry in my late thirties. Unlike P.K., who wanted to be a writer from a very young age, I had no ambition in this regard. My background was neither dramatic nor dynamic, and in fact, I was from a practical family and a Confucian culture. For a long time, I assumed it was accidental that I became a poet. But more and more, I saw it was destiny just as Page experienced. As Rumi says: "Not only the thirsty seek the water, but the water also as well seeks the thirsty." When Page was three, her family moved from England to Canada, then following her father's military posts, they moved again and again to Mountain areas and to the East Coast. These constant changes and moves stimulated Page's sense of restlessness and uncertainty. She started reading her father's books on time, life and death, then more books on psychology, such as Jung's *Modern Man in Search of a Soul*. From her teenage years, Page wondered about the concepts of reincarnation, the life journey, the possibility of parallel worlds, and the final affirmation of love. She started to view man as a traveller who could traverse time, and hoped one could be invulnerable like water, for "no knife can harm water…" I find personal resonance with these ideas especially her water metaphor since a water fountain healed me decades later when I started writing poetry in a dark time. Page's poems somehow remind me that the waves of poetry turn me inward to seek peace through dark times.

Page's life continually involved travelling and seeking. With her early years' reading of Virginia Woolf and Katherine Mansfield, she pondered states of consciousness and how to lead life as an artist. There was much she did not know, but she also acknowledged an unexpected entrance into the door of her mind. Page's father recognized her talent in writing and offered her financial support. With it she found some freedom and pursued her dream, and eventually became her own teacher to guide her artistic life. Her self-searching and teaching journey undoubtedly encouraged me to continue my poetry journey.

In 1957, Page moved to Brazil with her husband Arthur Irwin, a diplomat. There she found herself a total foreigner, like an infant, with a new language to learn. She described the process of growing up again, and she asked: "Who am I, the one changed by language, what is personality, identity?" [1]

When I immigrated to Canada in 1999, I had a similar experience. With a huge cultural shock and new things to learn, I felt lonely and helpless. One night after I read *The Emperor's New Clothes* to my son, a poem came to me. In the poem, a child turns to me asking "Who are you?,"... a sadness hit me ... I left China to come to Canada to seek a better life, however I found I was lost. The child awakened me and let me see my lost self. When I read Page's poem "Single Traveller," I felt it was very familiar:

"What is this love that is my life's companion? / Shape-changer, sometimes faceless, this companion. / Single traveller, I wander a wasting world / awaiting the much anticipated Companion ..." [2]

I translated this poem into Chinese in 2012, but today I still ponder her question.

In Page's later artistic life and difficult times, she used painting and poetry as vehicles for her spiritual and life journey. Her third poetry collection: *Cry Ararat* used her painting of a bird titled *And You, What Do You Seek?* for the book jacket. The same question I am asking again and again.

Although her life was complex and sometimes messy, Page continued sharing her love of arts and mentored many fellow poets. Although I never met her, I have learnt a great deal from her poetry, especially how to write glosas.

Her poem "Planet Earth," a well-known glosa that develops from a poem by Pablo Neruda teaches us that we must learn to love and appreciate the earth, a point of view which the world of today especially needs.

When Page died in 2010, she asked that half of her ashes should be scattered at sea. Perhaps she wanted to return to the original source where every life starts and meets again as in her poem: "The End:" [3]

We are the sea's, and as such we are at its beck,
We are the water within the wave and the wave's form

I hope one day my ashes, too, will return to the sea and we shall meet there.

Notes:

[1] from *Journey with No Maps: A Life of P.K. Page* by Sandra Djwa page 163

[2] "Single Traveller" from https://canpoetry.library.utoronto.ca/page poem5. htm

[3] from *Journey with No Maps: A Life of P.K. Page* by Sandra Djwa page 321

Patricia Young

Blue Monday

Walking the waterfront, I was thinking about
my friend who loved the world
but not too much to leave it,

who decided in the end
that music and art could not sustain
the body or bury the dead. I was thinking

about the dead, the unburied corpses
piling up in the Haitian sun.
How each day there were a few more

minutes of light. I was thinking about light.
The surprise of it, each January the same surprise.
On Blue Monday snowdrops dropped their snowy heads,

dogs lunged after each other in the leash-less field,
and I was thinking about tears,
more specifically, tear-drinking moths

that slide harpoon-shaped proboscises
under birds' sleeping eyelids. I passed a barefoot
slack-rope-walker balancing on a slack rope

strung between two trees and thought about my friend
who died in the house she'd lived in for more than
forty years, house her body knew as home,

and I thought, some deaths, surely, are better than
others. And the rollerbladers and the old ones
in wheelchairs and the babies snug

at their father's breasts, I passed them all.
Turning toward the breakwater, I decided to be
sad no longer. Besides,

what can you say to someone
who's packed her bag, put on her coat?
Sometimes leaving is doing what you want,

sometimes what you want is to walk out the door.
She left. Good for her. On Blue Monday
a cruise ship parked in the strait,

dumb as a thought,
and then for no reason
I remembered my daughter at three,

saying, I hate the stars, the stars are scary.
Then look at the moon, I said.
Oh, the moon, she sighed, I love the moon!

Yvonne Blomer

Afterword: The Legacy of Poetry and P.K. Page

And here you are, reader, at the end of this incredible book of poetry and art, reflection and praise, recognition and remembrance of the artist and poet P.K. Page. It has been a profound experience to speak with the essayists and poets collected here about their connections to P.K. Page and the inspiration she has given them. As for myself, I'm at my rather cluttered desk, poetry books everywhere, the spring sun and bird song just outside the window.

When I wrote the first draft of this afterword, we were in the throes of the dreaded Pandemic, and now we have eased into a near post-pandemic world. I'm not sure I can draw a metaphor between revisiting P.K. Page and her marvellous legacy and this pandemic we have struggled through, but I can say what a gift poets and poetry always is. I can be thankful for the paths, meandering though they may be, that have led me to poetry and the determination that has stayed me. So here I sit, with this book before me, my voice joining the voices of poets who are connected through P.K. Page, one of Canada's great poets, and I can again be relieved to have poetry in my life.

As for my own personal part in celebrating the work of P.K. Page, in 2011 I was asked to be on a panel at the League of Canadian Poets AGM on P.K. Page and to do a reading of her poems at an evening event hosted by Elizabeth Greene. This invitation came because I was, at the time, the Artistic Director of the weekly reading series in Victoria, Planet Earth Poetry, a series in its twenty-seventh year now. The series is named after P.K.'s poem "Planet Earth," with her permission. Until the café that housed PEP closed down during the pandemic, her poem hung on the wall for all to see.

I remember buying a fitted dress to wear at the reading and having friend Dvora Levin at my house to help me pin a scarf to my shoulders in a very P.K. way. I was nervous about the scarf as I lack the elegance of P.K. so that anything draped on me causes me to hook on doors, doorknobs or passing strangers. In the end, I wore the dress without the draping shawl despite Dvora's help. I wore high heels. I put proper makeup on. Most of these things are outside my usual habits, but I was hoping to carry myself appropriately, to have a semblance of P.K.'s grace, elegance, and commanding presence.

In this anthology, there are many examples of the glosa form, a form which allows a poet to borrow four lines and create a poem in conversation with those four lines, the original poem, and the poet. The glosa is a form P.K. excelled in and mastered, a form where she responds to poets whose work resonated with her. Glosas are the poet's opportunity to excel at emulating a beloved poet; that is, in this book, a chance to drape a shawl and walk elegantly, carrying an air of P.K. in their stride. Though there are many glosas here, there are also variations on the glosa, as well as poems that riff off a line from P.K. or a moment from one of her poems. There are other forms as well, poems that don't quote P.K. at all, and yet their shape or essence or even existence is thanks to her as a poet and mentor.

She was and remains one of Canada's great poets, outspoken and eloquent. For the P.K. Page tribute held in Victoria in 2016, *The Malahat Review* writes, "Immortality is not easy to come by, but if anyone has attained it, it would be Victoria poet P.K. Page." Immortality comes with readers and with writers who continue to turn to her poems for inspiration and for understanding. Here are poems that link back to their inspiration from P.K. and link forward to future poets who will have an opportunity to be mentored through the League of Canadian Poets P.K. Page Mentorship program.

In 1999 (at the age of eighty-three) P.K. Page gave a talk to The Canadian Writer's Union in Halifax. The talk is titled "A Writer's Life," and appears in *The Filled Pen: Selected Non-Fiction*:

> Although I have been writing since I was a child, it is only within the last year or so that I have owned to the title of writer. It was the day the surveyor for the city directory came to the door. To her inquiry as to my profession, I said, "Housewife." "Why didn't you say you were a writer?" my husband asked. "Well, you know how doubtful I feel about my own work. It makes me uneasy claiming to be a writer." He gave me a sharp look and said, "She didn't ask you to say you were a good writer."
>
> At that moment I realized that good or bad, I was, in fact, a writer and that I had been for perhaps sixty-five years.

I can't help but wonder, now, twenty-four years later, how P.K. would feel about this book and the subsequent mentorship program in her name. I'd like to think she'd be honoured, embarrassed, and keeping a close eye on us. No matter her own humble attitude toward the work she did, here are writers who connect to her work and remain inspired by it.

Since 2011, DC Reid has been fundraising for the League of Canadian Poets' P.K. Page Mentorship Program. This book is part of that effort. I came to the project mid-stream, after DC had sent out the call and begun collecting poems and essays. My part has been very much that of an editor, to select poems, contact the authors, edit and order the book into what it now is. As ever, it was a great privilege to work with the poets, essayists, and with Caitlin Press. There have been some delays, due to the pandemic and other unforeseen events, but here we are, book in hand in celebration of a wonderful Canadian poet and artist.

I'm grateful to P.K. Page for her vision as an artist and poet and to all the writers here who have shared their poems and stories of P.K. Page and shown her influence on their work.

We do not know the reach of our poems once we send them out into the world. Could P.K. have imagined this legacy? A book like this connects back to P.K. and those who influenced her, and forward to new poets emerging and curious about the influences on those around them. It clarifies how interconnected the dialogue of poetry is, through language and form. Here we share and continue the long conversation of poetry with P.K. and send it out to future readers and poets. Here we throw a finely woven shawl over our shoulders and walk into the world held by her poems and the gift of her presence in our lives.

Yvonne Blomer, May 2023, Victoria, BC

Open your door and step outside—the garden
becomes a Persian miniature—each leaf
discrete, the total petal-perfect.
So far, no sign of canker in the rose.

P.K. Page, "The Garden"
from *And Once More Saw the Stars* with Philip Stratford

Author Bios

Solveig Adair has been published in *filling Station, Dreamland,* and a number of anthologies including the Al Purdy tribute anthology, *Beyond Forgetting* and *Sweet Water: Poems for the Watersheds.* Solveig's poetry is inspired by the physical and metaphorical landscapes of the North. She lives in Terrace, British Columbia where she teaches, writes, and judges rabbits.

Rebecca Anne Banks, poet, singer, songwriter, musician, writer, artist, philosopher, counselor and activist passed away on October 29, 2022. She was the poetry editor at Subterranean Blue Poetry where she published poetry, critical essays, and art for the journal. She edited and published books of poetry, wrote book reviews, created social media marketing for books of poetry, created websites, translated poetry into French and offered artist workshops. In her life, she had over fifty projects in the public sphere, life ways books, CDs of music, Chapbooks and books of poetry.

John Barton's recent books include *Polari, We Are Not Avatars: Essays, Memoirs, Manifestos,* and *The Essential Douglas LePan,* which won the Gold Medal for Poetry in the 2020 eLit Awards. *Lost Family: A Memoir* (sonnets), and *The Essential Derk Wynand* (selected by John Barton) were published respectively by Signal Editions and The Porcupine's Quill in 2020. John lives in Victoria, where he was the city's fifth, first male, and first queer poet laureate.

Stephen T Berg was raised on the Canadian prairies and tutored by the West Coast. His poetry has seen life in staged performances, has been chosen to ride Edmonton Transit buses, and has appeared in such publications as *Prairie Fire, Orion, Earthshine, Geez, oratorealis,* and Vancouver's *Westender.* His first chapbook, *There Are No Small Moments,* was published by The Rasp and The Wine (2014), and his first full-length book of poetry, *Beacon, Blues and Holy Goats,* was published by Aeolus House (2019). For more of his work visit: growmercy.org

Stephen Bett is a widely and internationally published Canadian poet with twenty-four books in print. His personal papers are archived in the "Contemporary Literature Collection" at Simon Fraser University. His website is stephenbett.com

Barbara Black is an award-winning short fiction and flash fiction writer, poet and librettist. Her debut short story collection *Music from a Strange Planet* (Caitlin Press) was released to critical acclaim in 2021. Her work has been published in Canadian and international magazines including *The Cincinnati Review, The New Quarterly, The Hong Kong Review, Contemporary Verse 2* and *Prairie Fire.* She was a finalist in the 2020 National Magazine Awards, nominated for the 2019 Writers' Trust/McClelland & Stewart Journey Prize and won the 2017 Writers' Union of Canada Short Prose Competition. She lives in Victoria, BC. www.barbarablack.ca, @barbarablackwriter and @bblackwrites.

Yvonne Blomer's *The Last Show on Earth* was published by Caitlin Press in 2022 and in the fall of 2022 Palimpsest Press released *Book of Places: 10th Anniversary Edition.* Yvonne is also the editor of the highly acclaimed anthologies *Refugium: Poems for the Pacific* and *Sweet Water: Poems for the Watersheds* (Caitlin Press, 2017 and 2021). Yvonne is the past Poet Laureate of Victoria, BC and *Arc* magazine's current Poet-in-Residence. She lives on the unceded lands of the W̱SÁNEĆ (Saanich) peoples.

Marilyn Bowering is a poet and novelist who lives in Victoria, BC. Some of her works are *What is Long Past Occurs in Full Light* (poetry), *What It Takes to Be Human* (novel); and the libretto for *Marilyn Forever* (Gavin Bryars, composer). She has been short-listed for the world-wide Orange Prize, long-listed for the Dublin IMPAC Award, twice short-listed for the Governor General's Prize for poetry, and received the Dorothy Livesay, Gwendolyn MacEwen, Ethel Wilson and Pat Lowther Prizes as well as several National Magazine awards. Her essays have appeared in the anthology *Green Matters, Prairie Fire Magazine,* and elsewhere. www.marilynbowering.com

Kate Braid has written, co-written, edited and co-edited sixteen books and chapbooks of non-fiction and prize-winning poetry, in addition to numerous poems and articles published in anthologies and journals. With Sandy Shreve she co-edited the anthology of Canadian form poetry, *In Fine Form* (Caitlin Press, 2000, 2016). Her most recent book of poems is *Elemental* (Caitlin Press, 2018) and of non-fiction, *Hammer & Nail: Notes of a Journeywoman* (Caitlin Press, 2020). See www.katebraid.com

Poet and paper artist **Terry Ann Carter** is the author of eight collections of lyric poetry and five haiku chapbooks. *Tokaido* (Red Moon Press, 2017) won a Touchstone Distinguished Book Award and *A Crazy Man Thinks He's Ernest in Paris* (Black Moss Press, 2011) was shortlisted for the Archibald Lampman Poetry Prize. She is a past president of Haiku Canada and the founder of Ottawa Kado Haiku Study Group and Haiku Arbutus (Victoria BC).

An Officer of the Order of Canada, **Lorna Crozier** has published seventeen books of poetry, including *What the Soul Doesn't Want* and *God of Shadows*. Her latest book, published by McClelland & Stewart in 2020 is a memoir called *Through the Garden: A Love Story (with Cats)*. The recipient of many awards for literary excellence, including the Governor General's Award for Poetry, she lives on Vancouver Island and is a Professor Emeritas at the University of Victoria.

Sandra Djwa, CM, FRSC, co-founded the Association of Canadian and Québec Literatures in 1973 and wrote the annual survey of "Poetry" for "Letters in Canada," *UTQ*, 1980–84. Her biographies include *The Politics of the Imagination: A Life of F.R. Scott* (1986), *Professing English: A Life of Roy Daniells* (2002) and *Journey With No Maps: A Life of P.K. Page* (2012), which received a Governor General's Award. She is a co-editor of The Collected Works of P.K. Page and has received honorary degrees from Memorial and McGill Universities. She is currently working on "Living on the Margins: Country, Writing, Gender."

Wendy Donawa, Victoria-born, she spent three decades in Barbados as an educator and museum curator. She now lives gratefully on the traditional unceded territory of the Esquimalt and Songhees Nations. Her poems encounter historical ghosts, casualties of Empire, time's passing, identity, and that darned human heart! Her début collection, *Thin Air of the Knowable*, (Brick Books, 2017) was longlisted for the 2018 Raymond Souster Award, and a finalist for the 2018 Gerald Lampert Award. Her second collection, *Our Bodies' Unanswered Questions*, (Frontenac House, 2021) has survived the pandemic!

Margaret Slavin Dyment has a collection of poetry, *Travelling With Less Injury* (Quakings, 2018), and two chapbooks: *I Didn't Get Used To It* (Ouroboros, 1983), and *Tracing A Line* (Ekstasis, 1991). Her collection of fiction is *Drawing the Spaces* (Orca, 1994). Her non-fiction is *Travels in the Ministry: January 10, 2004–February 11, 2006.* Margaret Slavin Dyment co-founded the Victoria School of Writing. In 2000–2001 she was a writer-in-residence at Trent University, Peterborough, Ontario. She continues to write poetry and fiction, and articles for Transition Town and Quaker publications.

Patrick Friesen has published more than a dozen books of poetry, a book of essays, stage and radio plays, and has co-translated, with Per Brask, five books of Danish poetry. Their translation of Ulrikka Gernes' *Frayed Opus for Strings & Wind Instruments* was short-listed for the 2016 Griffin Poetry Prize. His play a short history of crazy bone was staged in 2018 by Theatre Projects Manitoba and was awarded "Most Outstanding New Work" by the Winnipeg theatre Awards. A book of poems, *songen*, was published in 2018 with Mother Tongue Publishing, and *Outlasting the Weather: Selected and New Poems, 1994–2020* with Anvil in 2020. A long poem, "Reckoning" will be out with Anvil in 2023.

Catherine Graham book *Æther: An Out-of-Body Lyric* won the Canadian Authors Association's Fred Kerner Book Award and was a finalist for the Trillium Book Award and Toronto Book Award, while her sixth collection of poems, *The Celery Forest,* was named a CBC Best Book of the Year. A previous winner of TIFA's Poetry *NOW,* she leads its monthly book club, teaches creative writing at the University of Toronto where she won an Excellence In Teaching Award and co-hosts The Hummingbird Podcast. *Put Flowers Around Us and Pretend We're Dead: New and Selected Poems* appears in 2023. www.catherinegraham.com @catgrahampoet.

A long-time resident of Surrey, BC, **Heidi Greco** writes in many genres: poetry, fiction, essays and reviews. Her two most recent poetry collections are *Practical Anxiety* (Inanna, 2018) and *Flightpaths: The Lost Journals of Amelia Earhart* (Caitlin Press, 2017). In 2021 Anvil Press published *Glorious Birds: A Celebratory Homage to Harold and Maude,* a book about one of her all-time favourite films. More at heidigreco.ca.

Janel Halenko lives in Nelson, BC, and spends most of her time with her dog, Muskie (named after the amanita muscaria mushroom). Even at work as a Registered Massage Therapist, Muskie is by her side. She has lived in Toronto, Cambridge, Victoria, England, Peru and most affectionately, in the Northern BC bush where she planted almost one million baby trees in eight years. She religiously attends poetry readings and currently self-publishes on AllPoetry. Her writing focuses on human bonding and connection, and in particular, how those bonds are able, under all odds, to fall apart.

Michèle Rackham Hall is an English professor and the coordinator of the Professional Writing program at Algonquin College. She holds a PhD in English literature from McGill University, where she studied the aesthetic, thematic, and historical intersections between modernist Canadian art and poetry. Her study of the artistic career of Canadian artist P.K. Irwin (a.k.a. P.K. Page), *The Art of P.K. Irwin: observer, other, Gemini* (2016), was shortlisted for the Foreword Indie Book Awards in the Women's Studies category. She has also published in numerous Canadian journals, including *English Studies in Canada, Canadian Poetry,* and *Matrix,* and served as a contributing editor for *The Maple Tree Literary Supplement* and *The Bull Calf.*

Marvyne Jenoff is the author of five books of poetry and experimental fiction with Canadian literary publishers. Since the early 1960s her work has appeared in journals and anthologies. Also a visual artist, she has used one of her watermedia pieces, "Hush, the Sibilant Rain," on the cover of her new poetry book, *Climbing the Rain* (Silver Bow Publishing, 2022). Born and educated in Winnipeg, she has lived in the Toronto area for most of her adult life. www.marvynejenoff.org.

Eve Joseph lives and writes on the unceded traditional territories of the Lekwungen peoples. Her first two books of poetry *The Startled Heart* (Oolichan, 2004), and *The Secret Signature of Things* (Brick, 2010), were both nominated for the Dorothy Livesay Award. Her nonfiction book, *In the Slender Margin* was published by HarperCollins in 2014 and won the Hubert Evans award for nonfiction. Her most recent book of poetry, *Quarrels* (Anvil, 2018) was nominated for the Dorothy Livesay Award and won the 2019 Griffin Poetry Prize.

Beth Kope grew up in Alberta, lived in Australia and Quebec and has perpetual wanderlust. She is blessed to live and work in Victoria, on the traditional territories of the Lekwungen and W̱SÁNEĆ peoples. She's the author of three books of poetry: *Falling Season* (Leaf Press, 2010), on memory and dementia; *Average Height of Flight* (Caitlin Press, 2015), a meditationon the solace of forest walks; *Atlas of Roots* (Caitlin Press, 2021) examines the impact of adoption on identity.

Leila Kulpas is the author of the memoir *Into the Eyes of Hungry: Growing up in the Wilds of Australia*. She has an Honours degree in English and a degree in Medicine, and specialized in Psychiatry until she retired, treating mainly those who had been traumatized in early life with psychotherapy and minimal medications. Her prose has been published in a Psychotherapy Review, a National Voices anthology and various newspapers, and her poetry on the internet by Pandora's Collective, in several literary journals and five anthologies. She first heard of P.K. at a Patrick Lane Retreat many years ago, and has enjoyed her poetry, and been inspired by it, ever since.

Patrick Lane has been acknowledged as one of the best poets of his generation. An Officer of the Order of Canada, the recipient of five honourary doctorates for his contribution to Canadian literature, the winner of the Governor General's Award, the author of a memoir, twenty books of poetry and two novels, he loved nothing better than gardening and taming cats. He died in March 2019, at his home on Vancouver Island with his wife, Lorna Crozier, beside him. His posthumous collection of poetry, *The Quiet in Me,* was published by Harbour Publishing in 2022.

Christopher Levenson is the author of thirteen books of poetry, most recently *Small Talk*, a volume of very short poems (Silver Bow Publishing, 2022). *Moorings* will appear with Caitlin Press in 2023. *Night Vision* (Quattro, 2014) was short-listed for the Governor General's Award for poetry. He was co-founder and first editor of *Arc* poetry magazine and for five years Series Editor of the Harbinger Poetry Series of the late Carleton U.P. After retiring from teaching English and Creative Writing at Carleton University, he moved from Ottawa to Vancouver in 2007 and was active, with Rob Taylor, in reviving the monthly Dead Poets Reading Series.

Dvora Levin is a former Director for Social Change Projects in Victoria and Israel, and now devotes herself to poetry. She has published six collections: *To Bite The Blue Apple; Sharav; Ragged Light* (Ekstasis Editions); *Zeroing In On Nothing* (a unique hand-bound book); *Windblown & Waving* (True Mint Blueprints); *Shared Motion: Science & Spirituality* (Ekstasis Editions). She has edited two poetry collections written by the homeless, sex workers and addicts in recovery. Until recently, she led weekly poetry writing sessions with parolees in a halfway house.

Dan MacIsaac writes from Metchosin. His work has appeared in *The Malahat Review, Event, Prism, Canadian Literature,* and *Pulp Literature.* Brick Books published his poetry collection, *Cries from the Ark.* His work was short-listed for the Walrus Poetry Prize, The Nick Blatchford Occasional Verse Contest, and the CBC Short Story Prize.

Alice Major has published twelve collections of poetry, most recently *Knife on Snow* (Turnstone Press, 2023), and a collection of essays, *Intersecting Sets: A Poet Looks at Science.* Her awards include the Pat Lowther Prize, the Stephan J. Stephansson poetry award, and a National Magazine Award Gold Medal. She served as president of the League of Canadian Poets and as first poet laureate of Edmonton.

Blaine Marchand's award-winning poetry and prose has appeared in magazines across Canada, the US, New Zealand and Pakistan. He has seven books of poetry, a young adult novel and a work of non-fiction published. His collection of poems, *Becoming History,* was published by Aeolus House Press in 2021. His newest collection is titled *Promenade.* Active in the literary scene in Ottawa for over fifty years, he was also the President of the League of Canadian Poets from 1991–93 and a monthly columnist for Capital XTRA, the LGBTQ2 community paper, for nine years.

Susan McCaslin is a poet living outside Fort Langley, BC, who has published sixteen volumes of poetry, including *Into the Open: Poems New and Selected* (Inanna, 2017) and *Heart Work* (Ekstasis Editions, 2020). She has collaborated with J.S. Porter on a volume of creative non-fiction, *Superabundantly Alive: Thomas Merton's Dance with the Feminine* (Wood Lake, 2018). Susan's chapbook, *Letters to William Blake,* was the first-place winner of the Mother Tongue Chapbook Competition for 1997, adjudicated by P.K. Page. It was produced on a handset press by Mona Fertig and Peter Haas of Mother Tongue Publishing (Salt Spring Island, BC).

Ottawa poet **Susan McMaster** has published some forty books, cross-Canada and intermedia anthologies, and wordmusic recordings with *First Draft, SugarBeat, Geode Music & Poetry,* and *Solace*. Recent collections are *Lizard Love* (Borealis, 2017), *Haunt* (Black Moss, 2018), and *Solstice* (2020). During two decades at the National Gallery of Canada, she edited thirty catalogues and founded the Gallery's magazine *Vernissage*. She is a former president of the League of Canadian Poets, and founding editor of *Branching Out*, the first national feminist/arts magazine. web.ncf.ca/smcmaster.

Originally from Vancouver, **kjmunro** moved to the Yukon Territory in 1991. She is Membership Secretary for Haiku Canada & a member of The League of Canadian Poets & The Federation of BC Writers. In 2014, she founded 'solstice haiku', a monthly haiku discussion group in Whitehorse that she continues to facilitate. Since 2018, she has curated a weekly blog feature for The Haiku Foundation. Her work made the Poetry Short List in The Federation of BC Writers 2021 Literary Contests & has been nominated for the Pushcart Prize. Her debut poetry collection is *contractions* (Red Moon Press, 2019). kjmunro1560.wordpress.com

Susan Musgrave lives on Haida Gwaii where she owns and manages Copper Beech House and teaches poetry in UBC's Optional Residency MFA in Creative Writing Program. Her most recent book, *Exculpatory Lilies*, was shortlisted for the 2023 Griffin Poetry Prize, and she is the 2023 recipient of the George Woodcock Lifetime Achievement Award.

Lynne Mustard earned her living as a writer and consultant who specialized in marketing communications. She also pursued a calling—training in and then teaching Mindfulness-Based Stress Reduction (MBSR). Now retired, she's turned to writing poetry. She has been published in two anthologies, several issues of *Island Writer Magazine* and she was pleased to receive a Cedric Literary Award.

Ulrike Narwani, of Baltic-German heritage, grew up in Edmonton. She completed a PhD in Slavic Languages and Literatures in Toronto. After living in the US, England, India and Thailand for many years, she moved to Sidney, BC, in 2003. *Collecting Silence* (Ronsdale Press, 2017) is her debut volume of poetry. Ulrike's poetry appears most recently in *The Antigonish Review, Canadian Literature,* and the anthology *Sweet Water: Poems for the Watersheds,* her haiku in *Last Train Home* and *The Wanderer Brush*. A poem has travelled on BC Transit (2018). A haiku won the 2020 Vancouver Cherry Blossom Festival Haiku Contest for BC.

Leonard Neufeldt is the author of twenty-two books, including nine volumes of poetry and three poetry chapbooks. He hails from Yarrow, British Columbia, which in his childhood was a hamlet of refugees and immigrants, most of them from the Soviet Union. His grandfather and father, under arrest by Soviet security, escaped and fled the country. Neufeldt has served in several foreign assignments and has conducted lecture tours at colleges and universities in China, South Korea, Germany and India. Avid gardeners and travellers, he and his wife, Mera, have retired to Gig Harbor, Washington.

Barbara Colebrook Peace is the author of two poetry books, *Kyrie* and *Duet for Wings and Earth*, both published by Sono Nis Press. She co-edited with Linda Rogers: *P.K. Page: Essays on Her Works* (Guernica). Her poems and reviews have appeared in various literary journals and anthologies, and she has read her poetry at literary festivals, in concerts, and on CBC radio.

Barbara Pelman is a retired high school English teacher. She conducts poetry workshops and is an assistant at Planet Earth Poetry's Friday night venue. She has three published books of poetry: *One Stone* (Ekstasis Editions 2005), *Borrowed Rooms* (Ronsdale Press, 2008), and *Narrow Bridge* (Ronsdale Press 2017), and a chapbook, *Aubade Amalfi* (Rubicon Press 2016). Her fourth book, *A Brief and Endless Sea* will be published by Caitlin Press in the fall, 2023. In 2018 her glosa, "Nevertheless" won the *Malahat Review's* Open Season Poetry Contest. Previously another glosa "After Winter" won the Literary Writes contest in 2005.

Zailig Pollock is Professor Emeritus at Trent University. He received his BA at the University of Manitoba and his PhD from the University of London. He was Principal Investigator of *The Collected Works of A.M. Klein*, and he has been directly involved in editing Klein's poetry, notebooks, and his novel, *The Second Scroll*. He has also written a study of Klein's work, *A.M. Klein: The Story of the Poet*. He was Principal Investigator of *The Collected Works of E.J. Pratt*; and has co-edited the *Selected Poems of E.J. Pratt*. He is Principal Investigator of the digital edition of the collected works of P.K. Page, *The Digital Page* www.digitalpage.ca and has edited *Kaleidoscope: Selected Poems of P.K. Page*.

Pamela Porter, poet and novelist, is the author of fourteen published books, including ten volumes of poetry and four books for youth, including two novels in verse. Her awards include the Governor General's Award, The Canadian Authors' Association National Capital Award, the TD Canadian Children's Literature Award, The Canadian Library Association Book of the Year Award, and many others. Pamela resides with gratitude on the ancestral lands of the W̱SÁNEĆ peoples who have stewarded the land for centuries.

DC Reid lives in multiple disciplines: web-based video-poems for his book *You Shall Have No Other* on www.sandria.ca; environmental writing, for which he has won multiple awards, including the National Roderick Haig-Brown Award; working on his ninth book of poems; won silver in the Bliss Carman Award twice, among many others, including the Colleen Thibaudeau award for significant support of Canadian poetry; his memoir of decades spent on the Nitinat River, *A Man and His River*, 2022, is his sixteenth book and won a gold medal in the Outdoor Writers of Canada contest for 2023. DC is broadly known for extensive work on the problems with in-ocean fish farms; neuroplasticity and extensive creativity mechanisms on his www.dcreid.ca site.

Joan Marie Roberts, a retired nurse educator, appreciates the vibrant and generous writing community of Victoria. She is published in a variety of journals and anthologies in both Canada and Japan. Her passions include kids, miracles, music and the joy of discovery.

Jay Ruzesky has published four books of poetry, a novel, a creative nonfiction travel memoir and articles, stories and poems in journals and magazines around the world. He is also a film maker and photographer and has been on the editorial board of *The Malahat Review* since 1989. He teaches at Vancouver Island University and lives in the Cowichan Valley.

Poet, editor, and visual artist **Sandy Shreve** has written, edited and/or co-edited a dozen books: five poetry collections, three anthologies and four chapbooks. Her most recent books are her poetry collection, *Waiting for the Albatross* (Oolichan, 2015) and the acclaimed anthology, *In Fine Form: A Contemporary Look at Canadian Form Poetry* (co-edited with Kate Braid, Caitlin Press, 2016). Sandy's paintings and photo art can be viewed on her website (www.sandyshreve.ca) or in person at her studio on Pender Island.

The late **Lesley Strutt** was a writer living in Merrickville, Ontario. Her writing has appeared in anthologies, e-zines, as well as numerous journals. Lesley edited the League's anthology, *Heartwood: Poems for the Love of Trees*, Canada's first full anthology of poetry devoted to the love of trees. Lesley passed in February 2021 with her posthumous collection of poetry, *Window Ledge*, published by Inanna Publications in September 2021.

Cynthia Woodman Kerkham has published in journals and anthologies; she won *The Malahat Review*'s Open Season Award and was a finalist for the CBC poetry prize. She is the author of *with feathers* (Kalamalka Press, 2023) and *Good Holding Ground* (Palimpsest Press, 2011), and co-editor of the anthology *Poems from Planet Earth* (LeafPress, 2013). She lives, and notices, in Victoria, BC.

Derk Wynand most recent collection is *The Essential Derk Wynand*, edited by John Barton (The Porcupine's Quill, 2020). He has published eleven other collections of poems, including his most recent, *Past Imperfect, Present Tense* (Bayeux Arts, 2010), a collection of fiction, *One Cook, Once Dreaming* (Sono Nis, 1980), and several books translated from the German of H.C. Artmann, Erich Wolfgang Skwara and Dorothea Grünzweig. For thirty-five years, he taught English and Creative Writing at the University of Victoria, where he edited *The Malahat Review* from 1992 to 1998.

Anna Yin was Mississauga's Inaugural Poet Laureate (2015–17) and has authored five poetry collections and one collection of translations: *Mirrors and Windows* (Guernica Editions, 2021). Anna won the 2005 Ted Plantos Memorial Award, two MARTYs, two scholarships from USA, and grants from Ontario Arts Council and Canadian Arts Council. Her poems/translations have appeared at *Queen's Quarterly, ARC Poetry, New York Times, China Daily, CBC Radio, Literary Review of Canada* etc. She read on Parliament Hill, at Austin International Poetry Festival, Edmonton Poetry Festival and universities in China, Canada and USA, etc. She has designed and taught Poetry Alive since 2011.

Patricia Young has published fourteen collections of poetry, most recently *Amateurs at Love*. She lives in Victoria, BC.

Acknowledgements

The P.K. Page quote at the start of the book from *Hand Luggage: A Memoir in Verse* (The Porcupine's Quill, 2006) is from the final stanza in the book. The second quote is from the poem "Presences" a glosa after T.S. Eliot's "Burnt Norton," and first appeared in *Hologram* (Brick Books, 1994).

DC Reid's editorial uses quotes taken from the following publications: *Journey with No Maps: A Life of P.K. Page*, Sandra Djwa, McGill-Queen's University Press, 2012; *The Art of P.K. Irwin: observer, other, Gemini*, Michèle Rackham Hall, The Porcupine's Quill, 2016; *Hand Luggage: A Memoir In Verse*, P.K. Page, The Porcupine's Quill, 2006; *Power Politics*, Margaret Atwood, House of Anansi Press, 1971; and *The Malahat Review*, www.malahatreview.ca/pkpage.

John Barton's "A Son's Nineteen-Seventies Wardrobe," from *Lost Family: A Memoir*, is republished with the permission of Véhicule Press and John Barton; its first line is the opening line of P.K. Page's poem, "Arras." "Illuminations" previously appeared in *Matrix*; "at the bottom of the field" is from Patrick Lane's poem, "Albino Pheasants," and "and I am lifted to a weightless world" is from P.K. Page's sestina, "After Reading *Albino Pheasants*."

Stephen Bett's two poems are from his collection *Broken Glosa: an alphabet book of post-avant glosa*, Chax Press, US, 2023.

Barbara Black's poem "Black Flag Warning" is a variation on a glosa. In addition to its regular form of quoted lines being the tenth line of each stanza, this glosa also includes four consecutive lines from a P.K. Page poem, each of which appears as the seventh line in each stanza. Lines are from *And Once More Saw the Stars*, Garden, II. P.K. Page and Philip Stratford. Stanza II, line 9 is a quotation from Herman Melville's *Moby Dick*, Chapter CXXV. "Consider the Pangolin" was inspired by the following line from P.K. Page's glosa "My Chosen Landscape": *…this shape without a shape/ is a violated country, one in which/ I am both exile and inhabitant…*

Yvonne Blomer's poem "What Tapestry" appears in *A Crystal Through Which Love Passes: Glosas for P.K. Page*, edited by Jesse Patrick Ferguson, Bushek Books, 2013.

Kate Braid's poem "Tree Song" was previously published in *In Fine Form: A Contemporary Look at Canadian Form Poetry*, Kate Braid and Sandy Shreve, Eds., Caitlin Press, 2016, and in *Elemental*, Caitlin Press, 2018.

Kate Braid's "Mumbai" appears in *Poems for Planet Earth*, Leaf Press, 2013.

Lorna Crozier's poem is from *Small Mechanics*, McClelland & Stewart, 2011.

Early versions of Wendy Donawa's poems "On Reading P.K. Page's 'Stories of Snow'" and "Aubade" appear in *Thin Air of the Knowable*, Brick Books, 2017.

Patrick Friesen's poem #59 appears in *a short history of crazy bone*, Mother Tongue Publishing, 2015.

Catherine Graham's two poems "Chthonic" and "Bullied" are *from Her Red Hair Rises with the Wings of Insects*, Wolsak and Wynn, 2013.

Marvyne Jenoff's "It's There" appears in *Climbing the Rain*, Silver Bow Publishing, 2022.

Eve Joseph's untitled poem appears in *Quarrels,* Anvil Press, 2018.

Alice Major's poem "Parting: A Glosa" appears in *Memory's Daughter,* University of Alberta Press, 2010.

Blaine Marchand's two poems appear in the chapbook *My Head, Filled With Pakistan*, catkin press, 2016.

Susan McCaslin's, "A Meditation on P.K. Irwin's pen and ink drawing *Winged Footprint*," will be included in her upcoming volume of poetry, *Named & Nameless*, Inanna Publications, Spring 2024.

The title of Susan McMaster's poem *Dorveille*, is from the medieval French, and in the derived English form, is a time of dreaming wakefulness between a first and second sleep, when many creators do some of their best work. With thanks to Frédérick Lavoie, who introduced her to this word at Banff in January 2019.

kjmunro's haiku beginning with "dark night" received Honorable Mention in the 18th HIA Haiku Contest in 2016, & was published on their website http://www.haiku-hia.com/contest_en/nyusen/18.html.

Susan Musgrave's poems "After Enlightenment," Not Enough," and "Tenderness" are from *Exculpatory Lilies*, McClelland & Stewart, 2022.

Barbara Colebrook Peace's poem "Dziekanski as a Map of Canada" first appeared in *The Antigonish Review*, Volume 184, Winter 2016.

Barbara Pelman's poem "Cello" appeared on The League of Canadian Poets *Poetry Pause*, February 7, 2023, and will appear in *A Brief and Endless Sea*, Caitlin Press, 2023.

DC Reid's poem "Love at Yellow Point Lodge" appears in *Love and Other Things that Hurt*, Black Moss Press, 1999. His poem "Nothing Better than Blinding the Beautiful" appears in *The Spirit of the Thing and the Thing Itself*, Ekstasis Editions, 2015.

Derk Wynand's poem "Sandpipers" appears in *Past Imperfect, Present Tense*, Bayeux Arts, 2010.

Anna Yin's poem "Purple and Gold" appears in *Inhaling the Silence*, Mosaic Press, 2013.

Patricia Young's poem "Blue Monday" appears in *The New Quarterly* and in her collection *Night-Eater*, Quattro Books, 2012.

The Editors would like to give a hearty thanks to Vici Johnstone, Sarah Corsie and Malaika Aleba at Caitlin Press for their amazing work on this book and for the sublime editing experience. We also wish to acknowledge the League of Canadian Poets, and the P.K. Page trust fund which will mentor poets in P.K.'s name. Also, thanks to all the poets who submitted work and donated to the P.K. Page Mentorship Fund. We are hugely grateful for your work, your memories of P.K. and her work and your poetry. Of course, our biggest thanks to P.K., may she be in orbit, her eyes still wide open.